PRAISE FOR *BEYOND ORDINARY*

What a moving and inspiring testimony! Justin and Trisha Davis are powerful examples of God's ability to breathe new life into a marriage that seems to have reached the end. With scriptural insights gained through the Davises' own fight to save their marriage, *Beyond Ordinary* encourages every couple to believe that their relationship can become truly extraordinary.

JIM DALY
President, Focus on the Family

Justin and Trisha have lived through extreme difficulty and brokenness in their marriage, but the Jesus we follow loves to take broken things and put them back together. That kind of deep healing has been part of my story, and it's the story of so many of the children Compassion is blessed to serve every day. I hope that as you read these pages, you'll find a deeper understanding of how complete dependence on God is the only way to fully live.

DR. WESS STAFFORD
President and CEO of Compassion International

Ordinary marriages are only one or two steps away from destruction, which is so unfortunate because the God of the universe designed marriage to be far from ordinary. In this book Justin and Trisha share a story of struggle and hope as they pull back the curtain on what was almost a tragic marriage, which turned into triumph because they were both willing to deal with the heart rather than simply trying to repair external issues. I am so thankful that they wrote this book and believe it will help people to stop fighting *in* their marriages and begin fighting *for* them.

PERRY NOBLE
Senior pastor of NewSpring Church

Justin and Trisha share their story with transparency and courage. But this book goes beyond just storytelling. They provide practical and powerful teaching that is applicable to every couple—newlywed or veteran. This resource will greatly strengthen your marriage. I can say that honestly, because it's done it for mine.

NATALIE GRANT
Five-time GMA Female Vocalist of the Year

Everyone likes a good love story. But many of us spend our lives slightly disappointed in the love story we're trying to live. *Beyond Ordinary* is what you've been looking for if you want to ignite your relationship to become what God intended for you to have. The practical advice and engaging writing will make you turn to this book's wisdom time and again.

LYSA TERKEURST
New York Times bestselling author and president of Proverbs 31 Ministries

My favorite thing about this book is that it's not a book on how to have a perfect marriage. It's a book about having a real marriage. And the difference between those two things is monumental. Honest, insightful, and helpful, this is an awesome resource.

JON ACUFF
Wall Street Journal bestselling author of *Quitter* and *Stuff Christians Like*

Justin and Trisha Davis have given every married couple a gift on the pages of this book. Their refreshing honesty peels back the layers of marriage to reveal the real challenges we all face. Their story will help you examine your marriage and learn what it takes to move it from ordinary to extraordinary!

JILL SAVAGE
CEO of Hearts at Home and author of *No More Perfect Moms*

Beyond Ordinary is raw, painfully honest, and wildly hopeful. Its rawness will cut to the depths of your heart. Its honesty will shock and shake you to your core. And its hopefulness will give you the gospel-empowered resources to have an extraordinary marriage and life. This book should be required reading for every Christian college student and church staff. It's that's good.

DERWIN L. GRAY
Lead pastor of Transformation Church

Beyond Ordinary is a great resource for any married couple. Justin and Trisha are courageously transparent as they expose the intimate details of their marriage in an effort to help others face their own marital struggles without being burdened by the overwhelming thought that they are all alone. There is a perfect balance of storytelling and biblical application that is sure to encourage every couple to strive for an extraordinary marriage!

JENNIFER SMITH
Author of the Unveiled Wife blog

In this book of searing honesty, Justin and Trisha remind us that marriage, like any other good and beautiful thing, is worth fighting for and cannot be won or kept without the desire to fight for it. In their story you will find your story, or you will find hope for a story that needs healing in its own way.

JOHN ORTBERG
Author of *The Me I Want to Be* and senior pastor of Menlo Park Presbyterian Church

Justin and Trisha Davis have given us a profound gift of transparency and practical hope in *Beyond Ordinary*. Through their own journey they point the way to better relationships and healing for all of us, whether we are struggling or striving. This is a great, realistic book filled with life lessons we all need to apply.

JUD WILHITE
Author of *Torn* and senior pastor of Central Christian Church, Las Vegas

Justin and Trisha Davis' story is more than just inspiring, it's evidence of truth. *Beyond Ordinary* gave us hope for something bigger than "ordinary" in our marriage and gave us the tools to see that hope turn into a reality.

TIFFANY LEE
Lead singer of Plumb

Beyond Ordinary is an inspiring marriage story that gives hope to those who want an extraordinary marriage. Justin and Trisha Davis fought for their marriage and won, and you can too.

KEN COLEMAN
Host of *The Ken Coleman Show*

As a pastor, I'm often asked what is the most important issue facing the church today. There are many, but in my opinion, it comes down to marriage. When marriages fail or stagnate, there is a ripple effect for years to come. Sadly, this is the usual, ordinary story being told today. That's why *Beyond Ordinary* is so important. Justin and Trisha are real people with a real story of extraordinary hope and healing. It's why this is no ordinary book.

JEFF HENDERSON
Lead pastor of Gwinnett Church

What an honor it is for me to be able to endorse a book I know will change so many marriages. As a friend of Justin and Trish, I have had the opportunity to see the way their teaching has spoken wisdom to so many others. I have also witnessed what a beautiful, strong relationship they share with each other. It is clear from my time with them that they love the Lord and seek to glorify Him even through their own brokenness, and I just know how many men and women will be blessed through their soul searching and solid, biblical teaching. I hope many people buy this book and move one step closer to that which the Lord desires of us: true restoration.

ANGIE SMITH
Author of *What Women Fear* and speaker for Women of Faith

We all want a life that's more than ordinary, especially when it comes to our relationships. But few of us are willing to pay the price, to do the work and go through the pain. Justin and Trisha show you what it takes—through their painful but beautiful tale of love and loss—to have an incredible marriage, life, and faith. Reading this book just might save you a few scars, but be prepared: it will also call you out of complacency and into something extraordinary.

JEFF GOINS
Author of *Wrecked: When a Broken World Slams into Your Comfortable Life*

Beyond Ordinary is the best marriage book I've ever read! Justin and Trisha not only share their heartbreaking yet redemptive story, but they explain how they landed in an ordinary marriage full of devastation. They share godly wisdom and practical advice that will benefit *all* marriages. Today, their marriage résumé has *betrayal* listed on it, but you'd never know it. They have leaned into their heavenly Father and allowed, even begged Him to take their once mediocre, deficient marriage and not only give them a new, improved, extraordinary marriage, but help you have one too. And you will, if you read this book.

CINDY BEALL
Author of *Healing Your Marriage When Trust Is Broken*

With touching transparency, practical wisdom, and biblically based advice, Justin and Trisha Davis provide a compelling look at the ways a couple can see their marriage renewed and transformed. *Beyond Ordinary* offers proof positive that even the most struggling marriage can be resurrected into a thriving relationship that glorifies God.

ESTHER FLEECE
Assistant to the president for millennial relations,
Focus on the Family

This is a game-changing book on marriage by Justin and Trisha Davis. Finally, a Christian resource for couples that preaches personal responsibility, facing conflict, and living with a sense of purpose and intentionality. This is a book that I will continue to draw on not only for my own marriage, but for the hundreds of couples I work with in my therapy practice.

Thank you for writing this book and sharing so authentically your story of how God refined your marriage.

RHETT SMITH
Licensed marriage and family therapist and author of *The Anxious Christian: Can God Use Your Anxiety for Good?*

Justin and Trisha demonstrate how to achieve the dynamic marriage God intends for us—whether we're experiencing catastrophe or just caught in the grind of the ordinary life. Every married couple should read this!

SHAWN AND TRICIA LOVEJOY
Author of *The Measure of Our Success* and senior pastor of Mountain Lake Church

Justin and Trisha Davis have an honest and heart-wrenching story about what happens all too often in today's marriages. However, their commitment to faith and forgiveness is so incredibly rare and *beyond ordinary* that it's an inspiring testimony of hope to any marriage in any condition. Learn from their painful mistakes, heed their practical advice, and inherit God's powerful grace through their story. This book will absolutely transform your faith in God and the future of your marriage!

RORY VADEN
New York Times bestselling author of *Take the Stairs*

BEYOND ORDINARY

BEYOND ORDINARY

. . .

When a Good Marriage Just Isn't Good Enough

JUSTIN & TRISHA DAVIS

Tyndale House Publishers, Inc.
Carol Stream, Illinois

Visit Tyndale online at www.tyndale.com.

TYNDALE and Tyndale's quill logo are registered trademarks of Tyndale House Publishers, Inc.

Beyond Ordinary: When a Good Marriage Just Isn't Good Enough

Designed by Jennifer Ghionzoli

Edited by Jonathan Schindler

Published in association with literary agent Jenni Burke of D. C. Jacobson and Associates, An Author Management Company, www.DCJacobson.com.

Library of Congress Cataloging-in-Publication Data
Davis, Justin.
   Beyond ordinary : when a good marriage just isn't good enough / Justin and Trisha Davis.
      p. cm.
   Includes bibliographical references (p.   ).
   ISBN 978-1-4143-7227-3 (sc)
   1. Marriage—Religious aspects—Christianity. I. Davis, Trisha. II. Title.
BV835.D383 2012
248.8'44—dc23   2012030588

Printed in the United States of America

18   17   16   15   14   13   12
 7   6   5   4   3   2   1

*This book is dedicated to our three amazing boys,
Micah, Elijah, and Isaiah. Your willingness
to pursue God allows our family to live beyond
ordinary. We love doing life with you.*

CONTENTS

FOREWORD

SOME TEN YEARS into my marriage, I found myself asking a question I never imagined I would ask. With haunting regularity, my wife, Brandi, and I were asking, "Why are we married?"

Several events had occurred that forced this question to the forefront of our marriage. We had several close Christians friends who were divorcing. Someone we really looked up to was caught in an affair. In our own relationship we realized that marriage hadn't taken away all of our problems; it had even added a few along the way.

Beyond that, I had bought into a damaging illusion that was eroding the very foundation of our marriage and causing immense damage. I knew you had to study hard to make it through college. I knew that if you were going to climb the ladder in any professional arena, it would require hard work and dedication. But somehow I thought that if you truly loved someone enough to marry that person, your marriage would just work without your effort and you'd live happily ever after.

So while I focused on trying to build a great church, I also unknowingly communicated to Brandi that I was perfectly okay settling for a mediocre marriage. And if I'm honest, that's exactly what we had.

I'll never forget the humbling moment when I realized that while I had helped bring Brandi some of her greatest joys, I had also contributed to her deepest pain. I don't know why I didn't see it earlier. I mean, think about it. Can you name any area of your life you can neglect and then expect to see improvement?

Does this work with your body? Nope. Ignore it, and you'll get fat.

Does this work with your business? Nope. Ignore it, and it will crash.

Does this work with your yard? Nope. Ignore it and, it will be overrun by weeds.

So why in the world do we think we can put our marriages on autopilot and they will still be what God wants them to be?

Marriage is deeply satisfying. Marriage is incredibly fulfilling. Marriage is loads of fun. Marriage is full of joy and hope and laughter. But marriage is not easy. Not even close.

Maybe you have picked up this book as a preemptive move. You're not in crisis mode. In other words, nobody is threatening to call a divorce attorney . . . but you know you're stuck. You realize that you and your spouse are losing ground. You're starting to neglect your marriage. There's distance setting in, a little hostility beginning to show, and you're not making any progress. You're tempted to resign yourself to the idea that this is the best your marriage can be.

But there's a little voice inside whispering, *You'd better do something*. I want to commend you for being obedient to that voice and picking up this book.

Maybe you are beyond "stuck" and feel like your marriage is on a respirator or maybe even flatlined. You feel out to sea with no shore in sight, and you have no idea which direction to head. As Justin and Trish are fond of saying, "There is a gap between the marriage you have and the marriage you thought you'd have," and the gap seems insurmountable.

But you don't want to give up. You haven't given up. It's why you've picked up this book. And I'm so glad you did.

Let me give you one word of warning: this is not a safe book. I know Justin and Trish. I know their heart. I know their mission. And with no apologies they're about to disrupt and challenge everything you've ever thought about improving in your marriage. At times this book can be painfully honest in its authentic portrayal of what can happen to the best of marriages when left to drift.

As soon as I started reading the manuscript that led to this book, I realized just what an amazing resource Justin and Trish are sharing with us. Tears welled in my eyes as I read, knowing this is not just a book that will help you discover an "extraordinary marriage"; it will actually tell you how to achieve it.

Much of the genius of this book undoubtedly lies in the reality that Justin and Trish have lived these principles themselves. I've had the unbelievable privilege of doing life with Justin and Trish over the past twelve years, and I am better for it. I can tell you firsthand that if you'll listen to the God-given wisdom they share in this book, your life and marriage will never be the same.

I am deeply grateful for the transformation that has happened in my own marriage as a result of the wisdom in this book, and I hope most earnestly it will be so for you as well. May the God of grace lead and guide you through each chapter.

Pete Wilson
Senior pastor, Cross Point Church

INTRODUCTION

A FEW MONTHS AGO my wife, Trisha, and I (Justin) found ourselves at the starting line of the Indianapolis mini-marathon. If we could finish the 13.1 miles, it would fulfill our three-year goal to run the race together. Trish had been training about three times per week, working her way up to longer runs. I had been training sporadically at best. I was counting on the adrenaline of being with thirty-one thousand running mates to carry me farther than my training could.

As we approached the four-mile marker, I got a huge smile on my face. We were running at a ten-minute-mile pace, and I felt really good. I said to Trish, "This is amazing. I've never run beyond four miles at one time before!"

"What!" she said. I could tell she was more concerned than impressed.

"I ran three times a week for the last month, but I only ran three miles each time. Every step we take past four miles is a personal best for me."

"You're crazy!" she said.

I preferred to think I was brilliant. "Think of all the time I saved not doing those long runs on Saturdays," I said.

Famous last words.

As we approached mile ten, I could feel my legs tighten with every step. I kept waiting for what everyone calls "the runner's high" to find me, but it never arrived. When we crossed mile ten, I went down. My quadriceps were balls of tightness, and I couldn't bend my legs or take a step without piercing pain.

My in-shape wife was just hitting her second wind but was gracious enough to stop and help me stretch. As I lay on the ground in pain, I said to her, "I don't understand why my legs are cramping up so bad. I drank water all along the way. I stretched out. I felt great just ten minutes ago."

"Justin," she said, "you don't train for the first ten miles. You train for the last three."

For the next three miles, we walked, kind of ran, and stopped to stretch when I needed to. Trisha could have gone ahead of me and finished in good standing, but she sacrificed her half-marathon time to stay with my ill-trained, broken-down body. We finished in just under three hours.

When most of us get married, we think we are ready for the race before us. We are optimistic. We are in love. We have a plan and a dream. We've dated for a year; we went to premarital counseling for a month; we read at least half of a "preparing for your marriage" book. We've trained. We've prepared. We're ready.

What most couples don't realize is that we don't train for the first ten miles of marriage; we train for the last three. Seemingly without warning, many marriages fall down in the middle of the race. Marriages that seemed fine a few months or years earlier fall victim to the grueling difficulty of the marathon. Couples who had every intention of finishing their race together either run at different paces or quit altogether.

Beyond Ordinary is written by two fellow runners. We've tripped and fallen along the way, but by God's grace, we've found the "runner's high" in the marriage marathon. This book is a reminder of just how amazing the journey together can be.

Beyond Ordinary is designed to help you along the way. It will stretch you. It will challenge you. It will inspire you to keep running. It will ask you to help each other up and to run with grace and purpose. To leave ordinary behind as you race toward extraordinary.

Ordinary is the biggest enemy of a great marriage. Ordinary is characterized by dissatisfaction, misunderstanding, and stale love. Ordinary is the birthplace of adultery. Ordinary is a place where divorce looks better than staying together. Ordinary is the subtle trap that convinces you that your marriage is as good as it will ever get. Ordinary marriages lose hope. Ordinary marriages lose vision. Ordinary marriages give in to compromise.

The way to an ordinary marriage is the path of least resistance. If you want an extraordinary marriage, you will have to choose it.

This book is a weapon designed to wage war against ordinary. It isn't about communicating better or learning what planet your spouse is from or what love language he or she speaks. Instead, this book is a transparent look into the lives of two people who have journeyed from extraordinary to ordinary to nightmarish—and back again, by God's grace. This is a book about the heart: our hearts, your heart, and the heart of every marriage.

If you're looking for a book that lists five easy steps to a great marriage, go back to the bookstore. But if you remember what extraordinary felt like and are determined to do whatever it takes to get back there, keep reading.

There will be times when it will feel like it's over, but it's not over. There will be times when you will be tempted to throw this book across the room. Go ahead—it can handle it! This book will challenge you to ask questions about yourself and your marriage that will be uncomfortable to consider. Embrace those questions and be honest. It is as we face our fears and learn to tell the truth that we begin to leave ordinary behind in our relationships with God and in our marriages.

Ordinary will be defeated with each turn of the page and with the belief that God is fighting for you more than you are fighting for yourself.

Welcome to the movement beyond marriage as usual.

1.

NO ORDINARY BEGINNING

FOR MANY OF US there is a gap between the marriage we have and the marriage we thought we would have. Sometimes that gap is created by unrealistic dreams and expectations. But more often that gap is created by a subtle equation that defines many marriages:

Time + unintentionality = ordinary marriage.

It isn't that we intend to drift away from our spouses, but over time it just happens.

Do you remember the hope you had the day you got married? Do you remember the vows you made—"in sickness and in health," "for better or worse," "till death do us part"? Your marriage was going to be different. Your marriage was going to be special. Your marriage was going to be anything but ordinary.

Is your marriage extraordinary today? Or are you miles away

from those early feelings, hopes, and dreams? Even the healthiest marriages have the potential to drift.

You may not be sure how it happened, but over the course of time, your marriage may have become ordinary. You are not the spouse you imagined. You don't have the marriage you dreamed of when you said, "I do." Words that once defined your relationship—intimate, fun, exciting, romantic, growing, loving, patient, forgiving—now seem to describe another time and a different couple.

It isn't that you wanted a marriage of mediocrity; it's that you've drifted into it.

Do you remember what it felt like the first time you met your spouse? How about the late-night conversations and the crazy things you did to impress him or her? What was your first kiss like? Can you picture the backflips your stomach was doing before you asked her to marry you, or while you were waiting to be asked? No matter how long you've been married, there is something special about remembering the extraordinary beginning of your relationship. It takes you to a place of hope, allows you to remember your dreams, and reminds you why you chose to commit the rest of your life to your spouse in the first place.

JUSTIN:

When I started college in 1991, I had my life and my future planned out. I had played basketball in high school, and Lincoln Christian College in Lincoln, Illinois, was only a temporary stop on my way to greatness. My plan was to go to Lincoln, play basketball for a year, take some core classes, and then transfer to a bigger, better school and play basketball on scholarship. I wanted to be a teacher and a basketball coach, and Lincoln wasn't where I wanted to be for the next four years. I was a late bloomer in high school and didn't get really good until my senior year, so my freshman year at Lincoln would serve as a nice prep year for bigger and better things.

A few days after I arrived on campus, the local paper did a story on Lincoln's 1991 freshman recruits. The article described each new player, calling me "the Cadillac of the recruiting class." That statement summed up how I felt about myself. I was the Cadillac of this little campus. My playing for them was a gift.

My attitude toward God was similar to my attitude toward the school. I was a Christian and went to church, but my life was pretty compartmentalized. Basketball had its place, dating had its place, and God had his place in my heart. I knew what I wanted to do with my life, and God could come along for the ride, but *I* was in the driver's seat. I had a plan.

Basketball season started, and I performed as expected. Lincoln had won eight games the year before I arrived. My freshman year we won eighteen games. At the end of my first season, I expected offers from bigger schools to come flooding in. I led the team in scoring and rebounding as a freshman; I thought that should be impressive enough. No offers. My plan wasn't working out.

I went home for the summer feeling defeated. It seemed that I had failed and didn't have a backup plan. I would have to go back to Lincoln in the fall. I started work a few days later as a cashier at Walmart in my hometown, Crawfordsville, Indiana.

As I was working one afternoon, a familiar face came through my checkout line. Kurt was a few years older than me, and his dad ran the church camp I'd attended as a kid. We recognized each other, and I asked him what he was doing in town. He was a pastor at a small church about ten miles south of Crawfordsville.

Then he said something that changed the entire trajectory of my life: "Why are you working here at Walmart when you could do something great with your life?"

My first thought was, *Dude, step off, this is only a summer gig.* I looked around to see where my boss was before I answered. "I don't know. I've never really thought about it."

"You should come be my youth pastor," he said. "I'll pay you a hundred dollars a weekend to teach Sunday school and children's church and to start a youth group."

Was this guy crazy? How did he get in my line at Walmart? I had no idea what a youth pastor was supposed to do, but a hundred dollars a week for a few hours of work sounded like easy money.

I went through the formality of meeting with the leaders at the church, and a few weeks later I started as their weekend youth pastor. My first Sunday I had eight kids show up for youth group. They ranged from fifth to tenth grade. I had prepared a message (my first), and it covered Genesis all the way through Revelation. The message lasted almost an hour. I didn't want to leave anything out!

At the end of the talk, I closed by saying, "Okay, if you don't want to go to hell and you want to invite Jesus into your heart, raise your hand." Kyle, one of the younger teens, raised his hand. I didn't know what to do at this point. I never thought anyone would raise their hand, so I hadn't thought through what to do next. Awkwardly, I said a prayer with Kyle, dismissed the kids, and then went to Kurt's house to make sure that Kyle was saved, because I didn't know what I was doing.

God used that moment to open my heart to his plan for me. I suddenly realized that I could partner with God to change eternity. I had never thought about that before. Over the next year, I would come back to that church each weekend the basketball team wasn't traveling, and God would use the church youth to mold me more than he used me to mold them.

My sophomore year, I didn't fall out of love with myself, but I fell more in love with Jesus and his church. I came to terms with being at Lincoln and changed my major to Christian education. Reluctantly, I was opening myself to God's plan for my life and surrendering parts of my plan to him. God was preparing me for the plan he had in mind.

That plan began to unfold in the fall of 1993, when Trisha and I met. I was a junior and she was a freshman at Lincoln. After one of our first chapels of the year, my friend Kenny asked, "Have you seen the hot girl with the bright red lipstick?"

I hadn't . . . yet.

I have to admit something: I am not proud of the story I am about to share. I wish that the details weren't true, but unfortunately, they are.

Kenny and I walked from the chapel over to the cafeteria, and there Trisha stood—big 1993 hair coupled with bright red lipstick. She was indeed hot. I wanted to make a big impression, so I approached her with confidence.

"Hey there, beautiful. I don't think we've ever met." She smirked with what was either charm or disgust. So I continued to wow her. "My name is God, and—" pointing to Kenny—"this is my son, Jesus Christ."

I don't really know what I was thinking with that introduction. Maybe because we were at Bible college, I thought it would be both spiritual and endearing. Trisha thought it was neither.

I thought it was money.

Trisha reluctantly shook my hand. "I'm just kidding," I said. "I'm JD, and this is my buddy Kenny. You should really get to know us."

Honestly, I don't remember what Trisha said at that point because I was so impressed with my introduction.

I knew I had made an impression. Kenny begged me to set him up with her, and the next morning, I saw Trisha walking out of the cafeteria. I approached her believing I could convince her to go out with Kenny. After all, I was a well-known junior all-American basketball player, while she was a freshman who, by now, had probably heard all about how great I was.

"Hey, Trisha," I said. "I'm sure you remember me from yesterday. I wanted to talk to you about something." She looked annoyed, but I wasn't fazed. "It's really early in the semester. Having been here a couple of years now, I wanted to let you know how dating works here at LCC. This is prime time because there are a lot of dating options right now. Those options tend to get less attractive as the semester goes on."

She looked at me as if I had a third eye.

"My friend Kenny that you met yesterday—"

"Jesus Christ?" she interrupted.

"Yeah, Jesus Christ. He may not be the best-looking guy, but he is really nice. You should consider going out with him."

Obviously this wasn't the best way to set someone up, but I was expecting that she wouldn't be interested in Kenny. I wanted to ask her out, but I couldn't do that to my good friend . . . until he was denied, that is.

"Sorry," she said. "I'm not interested in going out with Kenny. I have a boyfriend back home." "Boyfriend back home" was often code for "not interested." She wasn't interested in Kenny, but I walked away with an assurance that given some time, she would be interested in me.

I called her the next day to ask her out. Her roommate answered the phone.

"Hey, this is Justin Davis. Is Trisha there?"

I could hear her roommate whisper, "It's Justin Davis. He wants to talk to you." I was expecting Trisha to be excited to talk to me, but she sounded more confused than excited. Maybe she was just intimidated.

"Hey, Trisha. It's Justin Davis. I wanted to see if you'd like to grab some dinner, maybe go to a movie this weekend."

"Do you remember yesterday when I told you I had a boyfriend back home?" she asked.

"Yeah, I vaguely remember," I admitted.

"Well, I have a boyfriend back home."

"Oh, you were serious? That wasn't just because you weren't interested in Kenny?"

"I was serious."

"So me asking you out doesn't change your 'boyfriend back home' status?" I pressed.

"No," she said, and that ended the conversation.

She said no? I thought. *What just happened? Maybe she hasn't heard about how great I am.*

What she didn't know was that I had three guys from the basketball team in my room when I asked her out, since I was going to show them how to capture the heart of a lady.

I'm competitive, I don't like to lose, and my pride was hurt a little by this rejection, so I made a bet with one of the guys in the room that I could get Trisha to go out with me by the end of the semester. But even after my friend gladly pocketed my fifty dollars—way too many rejections later—I continued (unsuccessfully) to ask Trisha out.

But Trisha had made a fatal mistake in her strategy: she became a cheerleader. And since the cheerleaders traveled with the basketball team to away games, naturally, we began to spend a lot of time together.

TRISHA:

In 1993 I found myself, as if beamed from another planet, in the middle of a cornfield attending Lincoln Christian College in Lincoln, Illinois. It was a far cry from the hustle and bustle of living in the inner city of Joliet, just south of Chicago. It makes me chuckle when people talk about the "inner city" as this dark place in need of rescue. From my point of view, this poor little town in the middle of nowhere was in desperate need of some rescuing. For example, how can a respectable town have only two fast-food restaurants and one gas station?

I came from a high school with rich culture in which fashion trends were an eclectic mix of Salt-N-Pepa meets Nirvana. When I came to LCC, I definitely represented a fashion style the campus had never seen before. Cross Colours clothes and bright red lips were the norm back home, but it was apparent that Wrangler jeans and clear lip gloss ruled here. What else could these people wear when the only place to shop for clothes was the farm goods store?

I was the first in my family to go to college. I had no idea what

I was doing, and the fact that I stood out like a sore thumb didn't help. As I sat in my dorm room terrified, I thought, *I'm so out of place. I don't belong here. But I'm from Joliet! I'm strong and street smart. I. Can. Do. This!* So I stood up and went to the dorm room next to mine.

My introduction to a group of girls huddled together on the floor talking—who I assumed had all just met—didn't go so well. I was greeted with a look of "What in the world is this girl doing?" Apparently they *did* all know each other, and I had just interrupted their conversation.

"Hi, I'm Trisha Lopez!" I said. Why I felt the need to share my full name is still a mystery, but I continued, "Are you guys freshmen too?"

Crickets.

In my desperate need to fill the awkward air, I kept going with the questions. "Where are you guys from?"

Giggles. One of them blurted out, "Effingham, Illinois!" Now I'd lived in Illinois my whole life and had never heard of Effingham, which sounded to me like they were trying to say a bad word in code. I stood there speechless.

Eventually Jodi (who had more energy than all of us combined) spoke up and introduced me to the rest of the group. Angie, Jodi, Brooke, and Beth became not only my best friends but Justin's, too. Without my knowledge this crew became "Team Justin," his partners in crime to convince me to date him.

It started with plans of attack like Justin's driving to my hometown to a party that he wasn't invited to. Then there was the day he talked Team Justin into breaking into my dorm room to get my dirty laundry so he could wash and dry it for me, underwear and all. I was mortified!

Justin was the big man on campus. *Everyone* called him JD. Girls would rub his bald head and say, "Hi, JD!" So I called him Justin. I thought he was an arrogant country boy who considered himself the Michael Jordan of our campus. He definitely wasn't the guy you wanted washing your dirty underwear.

But something was changing in our relationship. The more time we spent together, his need to be "JD" melted away, and I was given a view into his heart that he'd never shown to another girl before. What he didn't know was the grander the view he gave me, the more my heart was falling in love with his. Team Justin was starting to win.

We started to share about our families. Justin was the oldest; I was the middle child, yet we both played the role of the peacemaker in our families. Our dads were both the blue-collar, jack-of-all-trades types. Our moms had both worked hard to advance in their careers. Justin's mom was a teacher's aide but earned her college degree to become a special education teacher. My mom was a paralegal who landed a job in downtown Chicago at one of the largest law firms in the world. There was so much we had in common.

Yet Justin was bold; I was timid. He could sell a used doughnut; you might buy one from me out of pity just because I lovingly offered it. He was book smart; I was street smart. My very first test at LCC was writing the books of the Bible in the correct order and *spelling* them correctly. It might as well have been the bar exam! Justin, by contrast, could glance at a textbook's table of contents on his way to a test and ace it.

The once-arrogant jock who relentlessly got on my nerves was now a friend I started to miss when we were apart. Rather than dreading his calls, I anticipated them. After turning him down fifty-one times, I was praying for the fifty-second!

I will never forget coming back to the dorm after my first official date with Justin. Team Justin was waiting for me in my dorm room. As I entered, we all giggled, and Angie, who was never shy with words, spoke up. "So . . . *what happened?*"

"We kissed!" I said as I slid to the floor with my back against the door, my eyes closed as if I were back in that moment. "When he kissed me it was like fireworks!"

Team Justin had won, and I'm so glad they did!

JUSTIN:

When Trisha and I were away on basketball trips, we would sit together on the bus and talk, hang out in the lobbies of hotels and talk, and sit on the bleachers and talk. We talked about everything: our families, relationships, God, ministry, our hopes and dreams, and everything under the sun. There was a natural flow to our conversation. Perhaps because dating initially was not an option, I felt a freedom to relax and be myself, and soon we became best friends.

The semester ended, and we both went home for Christmas break. We missed each other. When we returned to school in January, there was a sense of romance and attraction in our relationship that hadn't been there before. (It had always been there for me, but Trisha was now open to reciprocating.) Approximately the fifty-second time I asked Trish out, she finally said yes.

We went to Bennigan's on our first date. I felt like a kid on Christmas morning. I had a 1988 Ford Taurus, but I didn't want to drive that on our first date. I borrowed a friend's beat-up, run-down Chevy Cavalier convertible instead. It was January in Illinois, so we wouldn't be riding with the top down anyway, but for some reason, the convertible made the date more romantic. Trisha ordered a grilled chicken salad and didn't eat more than two bites. She was nervous; I was nervous. But despite our nerves, it was easy to be with each other. I had never gone out with someone who already knew me so well. When we got back to campus, I asked if I could kiss her. She said yes, and I'm not going to lie, it was amazing!

We couldn't talk enough. We'd stay up late at night talking on the phone. I was never much of a breakfast person, but I started getting up so I could see Trish in the cafeteria before her classes. We spent most nights studying together. We just loved being together.

A few months after we started dating, Trisha came home with me for the weekend. She was excited about meeting Kyle and some of the other kids at the church where I was a youth pastor. I could feel myself falling in love with Trisha before, but seeing her interact with the kids and share the love of God with them made me fall head over heels. We started to serve together. She sang and led worship for our little youth group, and I taught. God had created us to complement each other in an amazing way.

Not only did we fall in love with each other, we fell in love with the vision of what God could do through us as a couple. We fell in love with the thought of serving God—together. We fell in love with the idea of changing the world—together. God had brought us together and given us the same desire to serve him, the same desire to serve students, the same desire to help people find the way back to God through a personal relationship with Jesus. It was amazing. I knew I wanted to spend the rest of my life with this woman, and I wanted to serve God for the rest of my life with her.

I proposed to Trish on July 5, 1994. We had been dating only a little over six months, but we had been looking at engagement rings and dreaming about life and ministry together. Trisha was living at home for the summer, and I came up with a plan to surprise her. I drove about three hours to her house. I rented a limo and was going to pick her up from work.

Trisha worked at a Christian day camp for third- and fourth-grade kids. I got dressed in the only suit I owned; the limo came to Trisha's house to pick me up. I had purchased two dozen roses and had them in a vase ready to greet her in the car. As the limo drove me from her house to the camp, I cued up an audiocassette of our song: "I Swear" by All-4-One. This was going to be an *incredible* proposal.

I had called the camp director and asked that he keep Trish in his office until I showed up. He was glad to help me pull off the proposal. I rolled up in the limo, stepped out of the door, and the camp director walked Trish out of his office and into the parking lot. As soon as I saw her, my nerves went into high gear. I had made reservations at Michael Jordan's restaurant in downtown Chicago. My plan was to propose to her with our song playing as we drove to the restaurant.

Trisha was caught totally off guard. She was muddy and dirty and wet. I had had no idea that on this particular day the camp had gone creek walking. I was undeterred. I asked her to get in the limo. I was shaking as I pushed the tape into the tape deck and we pulled out of the parking lot.

I had my speech planned out. I had envisioned this moment my entire three-hour drive to Trisha's house. As I began, the driver took a sharp turn, and the two dozen roses fell off the seat, spilling onto the floor. The water from the vase filled the floorboard and covered our feet.

I was flustered. I dropped the ring box into the water. By this time, our song had played all the way through and a different song that had nothing to do with swearing or "better or worse" or "death do us part" was playing. Now *I* was ready to swear, just in a different way. As I scrambled to pick up the ring and soak up the water, we came to a dead stop in Chicago rush-hour traffic.

There was no going back. Despite the soggy conditions, despite the wrong song playing, despite my nerves and my unmet expectations of how this proposal would play out, I got on my knee in the back of the limo and asked the most beautiful woman I'd ever known if she would marry me.

Given how many times I asked her out before she said yes, I was a little nervous. But before I could even finish, she was crying and screamed, "Yes!" By the time we arrived at Michael Jordan's restaurant, we were engaged. It wasn't exactly storybook, but it was our story and we loved writing it together.

We were married in July 1995. After all that God had done and the plans that we knew God had for us, how could our marriage be anything but extraordinary?

TRISHA:

All girls dream of their wedding day from the time they know how to dream. One day they dream about the ceremony being inside at night with candles ablaze, the bride wearing a simple gown. Maybe the next day, month, or year they decide that an afternoon garden wedding with an elaborate, over-the-top dress is more fitting. By the time they grow into young women, they pretty much have the wedding planned before they ever meet the groom.

As soon as Justin and I were engaged, I put my plan for our wedding into place. I knew exactly what I wanted. I had envisioned every detail, from the ceremony to the reception, and as far as I was concerned, I had an amazing vision for my—I mean *our*—wedding day.

I am Hispanic. My father is Mexican, and my mother is German and Irish. Even though my immediate family celebrated only a few Mexican traditions, friends whose families celebrated all of them surrounded me.

One of my favorite Mexican traditions is a Quinceañera, the celebration of a girl turning fifteen. Traditionally, it's a ceremony that has many of the same customs typically found in a wedding reception, including a big, pretty dress. I love big, pretty dresses, and although I never expected to have a Quinceañera, I knew I would get an opportunity to wear a big, pretty dress for my wedding!

I envisioned marrying a handsome, tall man, and I never really cared what color skin God gave him because Alex P. Keaton, Ponch, and Theo Huxtable were all cute. I just knew he needed to be *tall*. My mom was about the same height as my dad, and she rarely wore heels. My man needed to be tall because wearing heels on my wedding day was a must. My tall groom and I would get married at the church I grew up in with flowers cascading over every nook and cranny. My dad would have to take one for the team and wear some type of shoes to make him taller so I wouldn't look like bridezilla next to him as he walked me down the aisle. My husband and I would drive off into the sunset in a convertible or maybe on horseback—as long as the groom was tall, this detail didn't matter.

Without realizing it, I did get the tall man of my dreams and the big, pretty dress to go with him. Imagine Cinderella meets '90s pop culture: the puffiest, most bedazzled dress ever created. Unfortunately, it wasn't just my dress that was over the top. My veil was so grand that at first glance, it looked like a bearded dragon. The man of my dreams could barely get close enough to kiss me without poking himself in the eye!

It was 1995, and that year the Chicagoland area experienced one of the worst heat waves on record. Still, despite the heat, Justin and I were set to get married on July 15 in Joliet, Illinois, at First Baptist Church, the church where I grew up. We were too broke for cascading flowers, so we cascaded cheap tulle instead. Our mentor, pastor, and friend Lynn Laughlin officiated for next to nothing, and my brother and two friends sang for free. Our wedding wouldn't be complete without Team Justin, who tearfully read Scripture and who ironically all wore black in protest that I was leaving them.

Even with the heat, I insisted on wearing my big, beautiful, and long-sleeved wedding dress and bearded-dragon veil. That would have been a very normal and appropriate desire for a bride had my church been air-conditioned. But it wasn't. A bride in a huge, long-sleeved dress in a non-air-conditioned church sanctuary with groomsmen wearing tuxedos and grandmothers on the verge of passing out didn't exactly live up to the vision I'd had as a little girl.

Thankfully, the reception venue had air-conditioning. During the reception, our moms spent most of the evening opening the cards we received, counting each check and ten-dollar bill in hopes that we'd have enough money to leave for our honeymoon. While they counted, I excitedly anticipated the very last detail I had dreamed of—the dance of the bride and groom and the father-daughter dance. Everything happened just as I'd imagined. Justin wasn't just tall; he was gorgeous inside and out. He took my hand, held me close, and danced me in a circle over and over and over again in the only way he knew how. It was endearing (and a little nauseating).

When it was time to dance with my dad, I realized I had never taken the time to think through what this dance would mean.

This would be the last time my dad would take me into his arms and dance with his baby girl. I had been so busy planning that I wasn't ready to say good-bye. I was barely twenty, and my heart ached for how I would miss not only him but my mom; my sister, Julie; my brother, Frankie; and my four-month-old niece, Kylie. Dad buried his head into my cheek and shoulder, and I cherished every second he danced with me—a moment in time that this girl had never thought to dream up.

As the dance ended, our moms were in a puddle of tears, not crying just at the scene before them but that we were given enough money to leave on our honeymoon. Justin and I were college students—broke ones—and we'd put every dime we made into our big wedding. Being told we had enough money to leave on our honeymoon allowed the sorrow of leaving my family to be replaced with gratitude that we were able to go.

We left the reception in a brand-new 1995 Astro minivan. Justin's parents graciously allowed us to borrow it. We had hoped for something a little sportier, but it was nice. As we drove onto the interstate, horns blared congratulations all around us. Exactly forty-five minutes later, we came to a standstill—one that lasted three hours.

Six hours after leaving our reception, we finally arrived at our hotel. We were simply exhausted. The carry-me-over-the-threshold tradition was abandoned, and all I wanted was to be carried to bed. As soon as we arrived at the hotel, "that time of the month" arrived too. This was definitely not what Justin expected! Instead of romance, he found himself making a trip to Walmart to purchase feminine products he had never purchased before. I was asleep when he returned, and being the gentleman that he is, he climbed into bed, kissed my forehead, and passed out.

We woke up the next morning believing that things would be better. Justin and I both grew up in lower- to middle-income families. Going on vacation seemed to us a once-in-a-lifetime experience. So getting to go to Holden Beach, North Carolina—

even though it took twenty-five hours to get there—was a dream come true. We'd finally arrived.

Although we needed a redo of our first night together, we thought we'd hit the beach first. The beauty of the ocean was overwhelming, and even more enjoyable was watching my newly married husband. Justin spent hours pretending he was dead in the water, allowing the waves to push him onto the shore like a beached whale. It was hilarious watching people freak out for a split second thinking that he was dead, only to have him pop up like a kid playing a trick.

We were so excited to be at the beach that neither one of us thought about sunscreen, nor did we, in the midst of having so much fun, think to keep track of the time. I was officially sunburned. Not just sunburned, *blistered*. We were on track to have the worst honeymoon ever.

Have I mentioned we still hadn't had sex? When your husband is calling his dad, asking what to do when you haven't had sex yet, you can be sure this is not the honeymoon he had in mind!

The last day of our honeymoon, I had healed enough to go outside and not feel as if the sun were going to melt my skin off. We decided to rent a Jet Ski. Yes, a Jet Ski—in the saltwater ocean. Justin was in the driver's position, and I held on for dear life in the back. To Justin's delight, we quickly approached a yacht that was creating some intense waves. He yelled over his shoulder, "Hold on!" I wanted to ask what for, but he immediately put the Jet Ski in full throttle and aimed to hit the wave dead on.

As I flew twenty feet *over* Justin, I heard the people on the yacht shouting, "Oh my . . ." I landed in full belly-flop position, and as I came up out of the water, the blisters on my face popped, skin was hanging everywhere, and I looked like a battered wife, not a newlywed on her honeymoon.

There is no question that our wedding and honeymoon were not as spectacular as either of us had imagined. But we were young and in love, and what brought us together was not only a love for

God and each other, but a shared vision to change the world for Christ. In the grand scheme, there was still so much life to live, and we were ready to start living it together.

JUSTIN:

When we returned from our honeymoon, I still had one year of college to complete, and Trisha was starting her sophomore year. She had taken a year off of school to save for our wedding. Trisha and I first moved into a cheap and roach-infested apartment, but we decided this was too much to bear despite its $150 price tag, so we moved into a tiny house. It was actually an old garage that had been converted into a house. It wasn't that attractive, it wasn't that nice, but the rent was $225 per month, which fit well into two college students' budget. And there were no roaches.

Shortly after the fall semester started, we found out that Trisha didn't have the flu as we'd thought. She was pregnant. The honeymoon was *definitely* over. We were four months into married life, learning to live together and to balance school, work, basketball, and college life. Our differences began to rise to the surface. Those little things that were so cute when we were dating all of a sudden weren't so cute: they caused conflict. I was a night owl; Trish was a morning person. I was a hit-the-snooze-button-multiple-times person; Trish was a get-out-of-bed-two-minutes-before-the-alarm-goes-off person. I spread things out on the desk so I could find them; Trish stacked things up so they looked organized.

One of the biggest fights our first year of marriage came the day we celebrated our first Christmas as a married couple. We were going to see our families for Christmas break, so we made plans to meet at home after class and open gifts before we left. Trisha had to be at work that day before I had class, so she got up first, got all of the gifts she had purchased for me out of the closet, and laid them beautifully under the tree. I woke up and saw the gifts under the tree, taking that as a cue to get ready for our gift exchange.

I went to the closet, grabbed the gifts I had purchased for Trisha, and put them in a pile on the couch. I made a nice little sign that said "Trisha's Gifts" and placed it on top of her pile. I grabbed the gifts that she had purchased from under the tree, placed them in a pile on the recliner, and made a sign that said "Justin's Gifts" for my pile. I felt a sense of pride in the accomplishment that I had organized our Christmas presents and they were now ready to be opened. I got ready for my last day of class and went to campus.

Trisha came home from work to find the presents she had meticulously placed under the tree stacked up in a pile on the recliner. She had no idea what happened. This was before cell phones and text messaging, so there was no convenient way to communicate to me, "What in the heck were you thinking, moving my beautifully placed gifts?" So she took both perfectly stacked piles of presents and repositioned them under the tree. She then left for campus to take her last exam.

You can see where this is going. I came home from class, saw the gifts back under the tree, and was totally confused.

Trisha came home from class, and I said, "Why are all the gifts under the tree? I took the time to stack our gifts in piles and to make signs labeling your gifts and my gifts. Why would you move them? That isn't how we do Christmas!"

"I don't understand why all the gifts are on the chairs," Trisha shot back. "The presents stay under the tree until we're ready to open them!"

"That's not how we do it in my family."

"What kind of family just stacks the gifts in piles? That's silly."

I then did what no man should ever do. "You're just angry because your pregnancy hormones are out of whack."

Trisha ran to our bedroom and slammed the door, crying. We were only a few months into our marriage, but we had quickly developed the skill to say things we knew would hurt the other person.

"You are being way too emotional!" Trisha called out to me.

"I can't believe you would get so bent out of shape over Christmas gifts."

"You're acting so immature!" I yelled.

"I can't believe you are so insensitive. How could you not even think about my feelings? You are so inconsiderate!"

"Inconsiderate! How am I inconsiderate? I bought you gifts that we don't have the money for so you can insult me about how we open them! That's *real* inconsiderate!"

"I hate you!" she screamed, and locked the door.

Hate me? I thought. *She* hates *me? How does she hate me? Don't we have to work our way up to hate? We can't start at hate! It should take years for her to hate me. Where do we go from here?*

The conversation was over. I didn't know what to do, so I took the opportunity to restack the gifts into piles to prepare for opening. It would be a few hours and many apologies before we were in a place to open gifts, but they would be ready when we were.

In this ordinary moment, gifts that were bought with love and thoughtfulness were now a visible reminder of the vast differences between us. There was a huge gap between the relationship we'd thought we had just four months earlier and the relationship that rose to the surface in the face of conflict.

JUSTIN & TRISHA:

GOD HAS A VISION FOR YOUR MARRIAGE

When a man and woman first get married, they don't yet know what they don't know. In fact, it would seem that most of us who get married think we know it all, right at the beginning. Trisha and I (Justin) certainly held the belief that our marriage would be different. That we would overcome the issues that plagued other couples. That we loved each other more than most couples. After all, we talked about our family differences. We could talk about anything. We knew each other better than anyone else knew us. Our marriage would be different.

There is no doubt that we all want our marriages to be anything but ordinary. The great news is that God has a vision for our marriages as well. God longs for us to see and experience the vision he had when he created marriage. Look at his vision:

> For Adam no suitable helper was found. So the Lord God caused the man to fall into a deep sleep; and while he was sleeping, he took one of the man's ribs and then closed up the place with flesh. Then the Lord God made a woman from the rib he had taken out of the man, and he brought her to the man.
> The man said,
>
> "This is now bone of my bones
>   and flesh of my flesh;
> she shall be called 'woman,'
>   for she was taken out of man."
>
> That is why a man leaves his father and mother and is united to his wife, and they become one flesh.
> Adam and his wife were both naked, and they felt no shame.
>
> GENESIS 2:20-25, NIV

God's idea is completely wild: "They become one flesh." We don't usually say "one flesh" in our world today, but God's vision for our marriage is *oneness*. What God calls *oneness*, we call *intimacy*. Often when we think of the word *intimacy* we think of it in purely sexual terms. Yet the word *intimacy* literally means "to be fully known." Intimacy, as God envisions it, is to be fully known by our spouses—emotionally, physically, and spiritually.

This passage reminds me that our vision and dreams for our marriages aren't too big; they are actually too small. We can't out-dream our Creator when it comes to our marriages. We often settle for ordinary when God longs for us to experience extraordinary. Genesis 2 shouts to us, "You're not crazy!" The longing we have for a rich and fulfilling marriage has been given to us by God. Our desire to be fully known and loved comes from a God who knows us fully and loves us anyway. This passage is a mandate for us to not settle for anything less than extraordinary:

ex•traor•di•nary
a: going beyond what is usual, regular, or customary
b: exceptional to a very marked extent

Maybe you're asking yourself, *What on earth does it mean to have an extraordinary marriage?* What sticks out to Trisha and me in this definition is the phrase *going beyond what is usual.* That most likely describes what your dating life was. A man might open the car door, think up unique places to eat, and always plan ahead to create time together that was even better than the time before. A woman might surprise her man by cooking his favorite meal, buying him tickets to his favorite game, or choosing to go to an action movie rather than a chick flick. Couples often wonder why it was so fun to date each other but why that same excitement feels so unrealistic for married life.

Where would you rate your marriage in the area of *extraordinary*? Can you think of a recent time you had an extraordinary experience with your spouse? If yes, what made it feel extraordinary? If your answer is no, what comes to mind as to why extraordinary experiences don't happen for you?

GREAT AT FALLING IN LOVE, ILL-EQUIPPED TO STAY IN LOVE

We are really good at falling in love. But what we see reflected in the divorce rate is that we are really bad at staying in love. We know how to get married happy; we aren't really good at staying happily married. There are a few reasons why over time we tend to drift into unintentionality.

The first is familiarity. Think about the car you drive today. Do you remember when you first bought that car? No one was going to eat in it. You were going to change the oil every twenty-five hundred miles. You washed it twice a week. You made the kids sit on plastic so they wouldn't mess up the pristine seats. But after a period of time, without even realizing it, you treated your new car as you did your old car. You stopped washing it twice a week and just waited for it to rain. The kids now eat snacks from yesterday's leftover McDonald's off the floor. Once the shine wears off, the glitter fades, and the familiarity sets in, you treat things differently. We do the same with our spouses.

The second reason it is hard to stay in love is that we live at a point of exhaustion. As we get older, our energy levels go down while our responsibilities go up. Marriage takes a lot of energy. It takes energy to listen. It takes energy to resolve conflict. It takes energy to put someone else's needs ahead of your own. It takes energy to raise kids. Because we are exhausted, we think we can neglect our marriages and stay in love.

But remember the equation we gave at the beginning of the chapter: time + unintentionality = ordinary.

NEW & NOT IMPROVED

We mentioned before that one of the things that helped us develop in our dating relationship was traveling together. Not only did we travel for sports, but each weekend we would travel to a little church in Indiana and lead youth group together. We logged a lot of miles. The drive from central Illinois to central Indiana in the winter is flat and open. There isn't much to see while driving back and forth. There are just miles and miles of cornfields between cities.

One Sunday while we were driving back to school, I (Justin) was not paying close attention to the road, and we drove through a flock of birds taking flight. Birds surrounded the car, and I found myself ducking (as if one were going to hit me). As I ducked, a bird flew right into the windshield and splattered feathers, poop, and blood all over. Now Trisha cares deeply for animals. She cares even more deeply for animals that die a violent death right in front of us. She immediately started crying, and I panicked. In a moment of insanity, I simply turned on the windshield wipers. That only smeared what was on the windshield, and Trisha cried harder. I tried to use the windshield washer fluid to remove what residue I could, and we drove back to campus in silence.

I bring this story up because it illustrates some moments we all face in our marriages: those moments when things beyond our control hit the windshields of our lives, when circumstances crash into our marriages and we don't know what to do. In an effort to make our marriages better or to make our issues simply go away, we turn on the windshield wipers, which really only make matters worse. It is easy to offer simple solutions for marriages that attempt to merely wipe away what is visible.

People are so much better at medicating symptoms of their marriage issues than at diagnosing and treating the root causes of marriage problems. We work on communicating better. We read books on anger management. We try to understand love languages. We listen to sermons on marriage. We go to marriage conferences. We try to wipe away all that is visibly wrong and fail to go deeper into the heart of our relationships. Yet we experience only incremental, inconsistent improvements in our marriages.

And we do the same thing in our relationship with God. So often, we would rather have God medicate the pain in our hearts than do what it takes to bring complete healing to us. So we learn to live with spiritual illnesses while looking for ways to make ourselves feel better. We go to church. We sing the songs. We pray the prayers. We join small groups or Sunday school classes. We may even give regularly. Yet we experience only incremental, inconsistent growth in our relationship with God. We do a lot; we just change very little.

The goal of this book is to move beyond the windshields of our marriages, to uncover the heart behind why the marriage you have maybe isn't the marriage you desire. Trisha and I want to help you see that the marriage you have is perfectly positioned to become the marriage God has in mind.

A lot of marriage resources focus on behavior modification. Communication. Anger management. Work/life balance. Money management. Improving your sex life. And we agree that these issues matter. It isn't that they aren't important issues to deal with, but most of the behaviors we struggle with are tied to broken parts of our hearts, and if we focus on the behaviors and not the root cause, we are not dealing with the issue, only smearing it around on the windshield. More information doesn't guarantee heart transformation.

We work really, really hard to improve our marriages by improving our behavior, and while these changes might last for a few weeks or a few months, we end up right back in the same rut. Even worse, we try really, really hard to improve our marriages by forcing our spouses to improve their behavior, and we end up frustrated and exhausted; and our spouses feel like they never do anything right.

Those in ordinary marriages believe behavior modification will solve their problems, that spouses can behave their way to an improved marriage. But you can't behave your way to an extraordinary marriage.

God doesn't want to improve your marriage; he wants to transform it. God doesn't want to modify your behavior; he wants to change your heart. Extraordinary comes when you, as a husband or wife, invite God to change *you*.

It is a dangerous prayer to pray—*God, change me*. You know why it's dangerous? Because this is a prayer God will always answer.

God longs to transform you. As much as you want to change your spouse, as much as you try to modify your behavior, God wants to change your heart. This prayer is where lasting change starts.

Will you pray this prayer? That is the question you will have to ask yourself before moving forward. Will you stop settling for ordinary and trust God for extraordinary? That is the journey Trisha and I want to go on with you. The great news for each of us is that God doesn't promise *improved*; God promises *new*.

QUESTIONS

1. Describe the vision you had for your marriage when you got married. How close are you to that vision today?

2. What are your expectations for this book? What do you hope changes for your marriage after reading this book?

3. What comes to mind when you hear the word *oneness*?

4. Are you more likely to pray, "God, change my spouse," or "God, change me"? Why?

2.

NO ORDINARY BATTLE

OUR MISSION to change the world began at a small church in Sandusky, Ohio. Not even a year of marriage had passed, and we were already expecting our first baby and beginning our first ministry. Barely in our twenties, we found ourselves serving a church in which most folks were somewhere between forty and ninety. It wasn't exactly the young, hip ministry we'd envisioned, but it was where we felt God wanted us, and we were eager to embrace it.

Our first youth event was a trip to Cedar Point amusement park. Only one student from our church showed up. Her name was Julie, and fortunately she brought two of her friends. That day marked the beginning of our relationship with three teenage girls who, along with us, embraced a vision that would transform the church. Within six months, the youth group grew to almost the size of our adult congregation. Students' lives were being changed, and we knew we were making a real difference.

From the outside, it looked like we had it all—from a young Christian perspective, anyway. We were broke, but being poor was just part of the package for fresh-out-of-college youth ministers. We were in love, expecting a healthy baby boy, and our ministry was thriving.

However, there was a darkness looming in the background that neither of us could see, a darkness that would turn us from partners into enemies.

TRISHA:

When we moved to Sandusky, I was only eight weeks from giving birth. Because we were both so young and naive, we decided it would be fine for Justin to leave for a youth trip five days after my expected due date. My mom was coming, and she had taken care of me for the first eighteen years of my life. I was sure she could take care of me for five more days.

As expected, our son Micah was born just five days after our one-year anniversary. *Thirteen* of our family members, from both sides of the family, came to stay with us in our two-bedroom apartment. Four days after I returned from the hospital, everyone except my mom went home, and Justin left for his trip.

I never expected the emotions I experienced while he was gone. Although I had given Justin permission to leave, anger boiled over in my heart every minute he wasn't there. As sleep deprivation and postpartum depression set in, Justin discovered a side of me he didn't know existed. Unknowingly, I allowed this frustrating and isolating experience to lay a foundation for my dysfunctional behavior for years to come.

JUSTIN:

Ordinary isn't a destination at which you suddenly arrive. Ordinary is subtle. Sometimes ordinary is a product of intentional choices.

But often ordinary occurs when a couple doesn't know what they don't know. That was the case with Trish and me.

We arrived in Sandusky in May, and I quickly developed a summer calendar for our student ministry. Trisha's due date was the middle of July, and I wanted to take the few students in our new ministry to a youth conference in order to build relationships and cast a vision for what I wanted our ministry to become.

We came home from Trisha's first doctor's appointment in Sandusky, and I got out the calendar. The doctor had told us that if Trish didn't go into labor, he would induce her. Knowing that gave us confidence to plan a youth trip for a week after Micah's birth. I would be gone five days, but Trisha's mom would be there, and Trisha assured me that she would be fine.

One of the things I've learned in over seventeen years of marriage is that the word *fine* is a four-letter word in marriage. When something or someone is fine, they are never really fine. I didn't know that then, and I took *fine* to mean, well, fine.

The week after Micah was born was so stressful. We were brand-new parents and had no idea what we were doing. We had thirteen people staying in our two-bedroom apartment. We were sleep deprived. We were getting advice from every member of our families on what we should do and how we should do it. My family was getting on Trisha's nerves. Her family was getting on mine. Tension was high, and everyone was walking on eggshells. Five days away couldn't come at a better time. My family left, Trisha's family—minus her mom—left, and then the next day, I left with ten students and two adults for a five-day trip to a Christian youth conference. I thought everything was fine.

After an eight-hour drive to the conference, we arrived and got checked in. I couldn't wait to call home to find out how Trisha and Micah were doing. I could tell when Trish answered the phone that things weren't fine. Trish was breast-feeding and had some discomfort the first week, but that day had been exceptionally bad. She was discouraged, Micah was cranky, and I was eight hours away. I got the sense that she didn't miss me; she was just mad at me for being gone.

"I'm sorry that Micah is having trouble eating," I said.

"It's fine."

"Well, remember what we talked about. We don't have the money to buy formula, so you need to breast-feed as long as you can."

"I know! Why are you reminding me of something I already know? Do you think I'm trying to make feeding difficult? Do you think I'm intentionally causing it to hurt? Is that what you think?"

"No, I don't think that at all. I was just saying that we don't have the money for this not to work."

Silence.

"I'll let you go so you can get back to the students," she said, icily.

"The students are fine. I want to talk to you."

Silence.

I could hear sniffling that she tried to contain. I could picture the tears streaming down her cheeks.

"I just can't believe you would leave us a week after Micah was born." She spoke quietly, almost as if she were talking to herself and allowing me to hear.

"You said it would be fine," I reminded her. "You said your mom would be there and it was only five days. I didn't leave you; I just went on a trip with students for *my job*. I'm sorry that I have a job and am trying to provide for our family."

Silence.

"I guess I'll let you go," one of us said.

"Okay," replied the other.

When we hung up the phone that night, a seed was planted in both of our hearts. We weren't in this together anymore. In Trisha's mind I was the enemy. I had left her. I had deserted her and our newborn baby. I wanted to be with the students more than I wanted to be with her.

To me, she wasn't supporting me as she should. She went back on her word, and what she said would be fine wasn't fine anymore. She was mad at me for working. She was mad at me for providing. She was mad at me for doing something she told me I could do.

We had spent our entire dating life serving God together, and now, just a few months into our first full-time ministry and just a year into our marriage, I felt as if I and my ministry were on one side and she was on the other. The field had been set for us to move from teammates to enemies.

TRISHA:

When Justin and I got married, we had a vision that we would do life together and would change the world together through our ministry in the local church. But what slowly took place was a shift in our posture of doing life and ministry together, and we began to complain about how the other person needed to change. We went from "I love you so much; how can I serve you?" to "If you loved me, then you would do this for me."

We were now parents and were at a church where Micah was, seriously, the only baby in the entire church. Although I felt welcome at our new church, there wasn't one person I could connect with who was in my season of life or who was even my age, for that matter. I felt all alone.

I was struggling with how to be Justin's partner in ministry now that we had a baby. When Justin left for that youth conference just days after Micah was born, I felt like he didn't care that I wasn't with him. I couldn't just pop in and out of the office. I couldn't lead a small group or sing at church whenever I was needed because everything required a babysitter. We could barely pay the bills, let alone a sitter.

Neither Justin nor I knew this wave of change would bring about so much internal chaos for both of us. Instead of believing Justin was fighting for me, I slowly began to make him the enemy simply for not involving me in his life in the way I was used to.

I convinced myself that the only way he would value me as his wife and want to continue to be my husband was if I was doing ministry with him.

This was my insanity.

I was a twenty-one-year-old with an infant whose husband now worked full time, and I did not have one friend nearby to lean on. I missed Justin. I missed Team Justin, and I missed being young. I longed for friends—or at least *a* friend—I could enjoy this stage of life with, but Justin was the only person I knew. I was desperate for community. It made the ache to be closer to my family grow stronger by the day.

I'll never forget the day that Gary and Andrea Keener walked into our small church. They were our age, newly married, and had *BFF* written all over them! I ran up to them and introduced myself. They told me their names, and just like that, the college Trisha who had walked into a dorm room full of girls she didn't know barraged them with questions. It was friendship at first sight.

Gary and Dre (as I call her) were junior high sweethearts who grew up in the sticks of Ohio and loved everything about farm life. They moved to Sandusky for teaching positions: Dre taught home economics and Gary taught shop. She is bold, speaks her mind, and can cook Bobby Flay under the table, and she has a loyalty and trustworthy character to match. Gary is sweet, soft spoken, and can make or fix anything.

The four of us could not have been more different in personality or gifting, but what we did have in common was a passion to love others. God had heard Justin's and my cries and gave us the gift of community through the Keeners. We moved—for the fourth time—from our old apartment into an apartment right across the hall from theirs. It was as if we were back in the dorms with friends close by. It's a friendship we are still blessed by to this day.

Life was starting to feel balanced again. I wasn't putting as much pressure on Justin to come home every day for lunch. We both had another outlet for community, and Gary and Andrea seemed to bring out the best in us. Although they didn't yet have children, it was a someday dream for them, and they loved living vicariously through us yet still getting to sleep through the night. Life was good—I thought.

JUSTIN:

A year after Micah was born, my parents invited us to go on vacation with them to Florida. I didn't think I should take vacation time so early into my new job, but this seemed like the break that Trisha needed. My family could help watch Micah, and Trish could have some relaxation time to herself. So Trisha and Micah flew from Ohio to Florida to spend the week on vacation with my parents.

About halfway through the week, I got a call from Trisha's mom. The way Trisha's mom said my name when I answered the phone, I knew something was wrong. She asked if Trisha was available, and I told her that Trish was with my parents in Florida on vacation. Trisha had called her mom earlier in the week to let her know of her plans, so this made the phone call even more bizarre. I asked what was wrong and if I could do anything to help. My mother-in-law shared with me the decision that she and Trisha's dad had made to get divorced after twenty-five years of marriage. She was crying, I was crying, and all I could think about was how devastated Trisha would be when she found out.

Trisha's mom was a wreck, and she didn't know whether she would be able to emotionally handle having this conversation with Trisha. She asked me if I would tell Trisha. I told my mother-in-law that I would do that. We both decided that my telling Trisha over the phone wouldn't be the best choice. I would tell her when she got back to Ohio.

Two days later I picked up Trish and Micah from the airport in Cleveland, knowing we had an hour's drive from the airport back to our house. I would use this time to explain to her what her mom had shared with me, and then she could call her mom when we got home.

"I need to tell you something," I said as we left the airport.

"Okay. What is it? What's wrong? Just tell me," she said, knowing something was off.

"Your mom called a couple of days ago and told me that she and your dad are getting divorced. I'm really sorry, but she didn't want to tell you over the phone. She asked—"

"What! Are you kidding me? Divorced! You have to be kidding!" She began to cry. Micah began to cry. She was devastated. She was reacting just as I thought she would—until she started yelling at me.

"This is all your fault!" she said. "You moved me away from my family! You moved me six hours away. I wasn't there for them when they needed me most, and it's all your fault!"

My fault? My fault! I couldn't believe what I was hearing. "I didn't move you away from your family. I *saved* you from your family! I rescued you. You should be grateful to me, not mad at me!"

Silence.

Instead of being there for her, I was resentful. Instead of looking to me for comfort, she looked at me with blame. We were no longer working with each other; we were blaming each other. This event began to shape our marriage in ways we didn't realize at the time. We got really good not at fighting *for* each other but instead at fighting *with* each other. We were good at being enemies.

TRISHA:

After being on vacation with Justin's family, my young husband told me my parents, whom I'd only known as married and in love, were no longer either. I was shocked, heartbroken, and angry. The life, community, and ministry we had spent the past year building felt shattered in one conversation. If my parents' marriage couldn't last, then how would Justin and I last?

This thought process slowly ate away at my heart like a cancer, spreading into other areas of my life. In my effort to control Justin to protect myself, I was only pushing him away. We both started to believe that our marriage would be better if the other would change.

We became so accustomed to living like this that I had convinced myself that I was actually right all the time, and Justin was convinced I could never handle his true feelings and struggles. It was a cycle that crippled our marriage. We would make up and play nice for a while, but before long we would find ourselves fighting again over the same things we had always fought about. This dysfunction eventually became our normal way of married life.

JUSTIN & TRISHA:

ONENESS BROKEN

God designed and created us to be known by him and to be one with our spouses. That is his vision for marriage. That is his desire. But there has been a war against that oneness since the Garden of Eden. The initial battle in the Garden was lost, and oneness was broken:

> The serpent was the shrewdest of all the wild animals the LORD God had made. One day he asked the woman, "Did God really say you must not eat the fruit from any of the trees in the garden?"
>
> "Of course we may eat fruit from the trees in the garden," the woman replied. "It's only the fruit from the tree in the middle of the garden that we are not allowed to eat. God said, 'You must not eat it or even touch it; if you do, you will die.'"
>
> "You won't die!" the serpent replied to the woman. "God knows that your eyes will be opened as soon as you eat it, and you will be like God, knowing both good and evil."

The woman was convinced. She saw that the tree was beautiful and its fruit looked delicious, and she wanted the wisdom it would give her. So she took some of the fruit and ate it. Then she gave some to her husband, who was with her, and he ate it, too.

GENESIS 3:1-6

We know the story of Adam and Eve. For some of us, we've heard it so often that it has lost its punch. At a glance, it's a story that seems black and white. Adam and Eve eat the fruit, and there are consequences. But if we look closer, we see layers of dysfunction that provide a road map to the breaking of intimacy—not only in Adam and Eve's relationship, but also in our own marriage relationships.

In verse one, the first spiritual battle takes place. Satan moves in on the human relationship with a simple question: "Did God really say . . . ?" From the very beginning, Satan tapped into an unspoken fear that we as humans have: *God is holding out on us.* When we start questioning God's provision, God's goodness, and God's plan, it is easy to question God's Word. "Did God really say . . . ?" Eve's choice to believe God was holding out on her broke intimacy between her and God and between her and Adam.

Think about your own relationships. Can you remember a time when "Did God really say . . . ?" broke intimacy in your relationship with your spouse? It may not be a question that involves eating fruit, but Satan is shrewd and knows which questions to provoke you to ask yourself. Maybe your questions go something like this:

- "Did God really say I have to respect my husband even though he's disrespectful to me?"
- "Did God really say that I should love my wife as Christ loves the church even though she gives her best to everyone but me?"
- "Did God really say to not let the sun go down on my anger?"
- "Did God really say to be slow to speak and quick to listen?"

In Satan's attempt to trip up Eve, he simply posed a question and left Eve to answer it herself. Satan knew the effect the question would have on Eve. In that moment, Eve was focused on her own needs rather than taking the time to pose her own question, like, "Will my actions draw me closer to God or closer to my husband?" Often it's the small, simple, it's-just-a-piece-of-fruit moments in our marriage relationships that can cause the most damage as we think only about what's best for ourselves.

THE ENEMY OF ONENESS

Last October, our family was given free rein of a beach house in Florida during our kids' fall break. We had a blast playing on the beach and swimming in the clear ocean water. About halfway through our second day, I (Justin) started feeling numerous stings all over my legs and feet. I am somewhat of a hypochondriac, and my family tends to make fun of me at times for my tendency to believe I am dying from illnesses that don't even exist. So there was no way I was going to share the stinging sensation I felt in my legs. As the discomfort became more intense for me, my kids said that they were feeling something too. I was just pumped that I wasn't crazy.

Just then, this David Hasselhoff–looking guy came running down the beach toward us. He stopped by me and pulled his swim trunks up from his knee toward his upper thigh—honestly a little higher than I was comfortable seeing. On his thigh was a huge welt. Inside a bucket he was carrying a huge jellyfish. As we looked around, we noticed literally hundreds of tiny jellyfish in the water and washing up on the shore. The truth is that these jellyfish had been in the water the entire time; we only noticed them when they started stinging us.

That is how spiritual warfare works. There is a battle for your marriage all day, every day. Most of the time we only notice it after we get stung.

Marriage is physical and emotional, but more than anything

else, marriage is spiritual. We have an enemy who seeks to steal our hearts, kill our hope, and destroy our marriages. Our struggle against this enemy is what we know as spiritual warfare.

Spiritual warfare isn't something we talk about very much, especially as it relates to marriage. We see it most often as something TV preachers exploit, or something crazy guys talk about when they're claiming the end of the world is near. But just because I don't understand spiritual warfare and just because I don't always acknowledge spiritual warfare doesn't mean it doesn't exist.

Maybe what you need to move past ordinary is to recognize the war being fought against you right now. God longs to shift the momentum of your marriage, and often that shift is found in recognizing the battle that your marriage is fighting every single day.

From the very beginning, there has been a war waged against oneness. Satan's mission was to destroy the intimacy Adam and Eve experienced with God and to destroy the oneness that God had created them to experience with one another. With one act, both were destroyed. The momentum of their marriage shifted. The result of their choice was hiding and blaming.

Look at Genesis 3:7-8: "At that moment their eyes were opened, and they suddenly felt shame at their nakedness. So they sewed fig leaves together to cover themselves. When the cool evening breezes were blowing, the man and his wife heard the LORD God walking about in the garden. So they hid from the LORD God among the trees."

Adam and Eve's first response after succumbing to temptation was to hide. For the first time, they felt shame. For the first time, they felt as if who they were wasn't good enough and that they needed to cover up. They were exposed, vulnerable. They were naked, and they knew it. So they covered up and hid from each other. When they heard God, they knew they were caught, so they hid from him, as well.

One of the biggest enemies to extraordinary oneness is the desire to hide.

When we get married, we truly believe that the person we marry knows us better than anyone else. We have a desire to share our entire life with him or her. But as we go through life, we become tempted to hide. We feel ashamed, and we grab our fig leaves because we aren't comfortable being exposed—even to our spouses.

Somewhere along the way, we convince ourselves that we can hide from God, as well. If we attend church enough, if we pray enough, if we read our Bibles enough, then we think we can withhold parts of our hearts from God and this hiding won't affect us. But hiding withers away the oneness that God longs to experience with us.

In the Genesis passage, God finds Adam and Eve (as if they were ever really lost), and Adam does something that married couples tend to do when problems are exposed: he blames his spouse. "The man replied, 'It was the woman you gave me who gave me the fruit, and I ate it'" (Genesis 3:12).

Wait, who's the enemy again? Your spouse? No—we have one enemy, and when we blame each other, we become victims in our marriages rather than partners.

Maybe that describes your marriage today. Maybe it feels easier to hide from your spouse than to spend time with him or her. Everything that happens in your marriage is the other person's fault. Even though you know you have a share of the blame, you find it much easier to shift blame than to take responsibility. You are both victims, not partners. Trisha and I lived like this for years, and it almost destroyed our marriage.

But God created us to be one with our spouses. Anything short of that is merely ordinary.

HOW WE TRY TO RESTORE ONENESS

When our marriages drift toward ordinary, we often try to roll up our sleeves and fix them ourselves. We won't go down without a fight. We'll come up with a plan. We are going to make our marriages better. We are going to try harder. We truly believe we can restore oneness. We try to better our marriages ourselves in three (misguided) ways.

I Can Change You

If we are honest, probably all of us think we can change our spouses. Ladies, you truly believe that you can make your husband a better driver. You can make him more punctual. You can make him put his dirty underwear *in* the hamper instead of *next to* the hamper. If you complain enough, nag enough, and pout enough, you will be able to change your husband into the man you thought he was when you married him.

Guys, you believe you can change your wife. You truly think that you can make your wife want sex as often as you do. You think you can make her want to watch Chuck Norris movies. You really believe that if you are good enough or on time enough or clean enough, then she won't get sideways when you go golfing on Saturdays.

The truth is this: *we can't change our spouses.*

None of us has the capacity to change a human heart. We think that by trying to change our spouses' behavior we are changing their hearts, but that isn't true. By trying to change our spouses' behavior we are actually damaging their hearts. So many marriages exist full of bitterness and hurt. Why? Because we believe we can restore oneness by changing our spouses. One spouse is upset that he or she is never good enough; the other feels like all he or she does is nag and complain. Oneness slips further and further away.

Milestones & Achievements

Another way we try to restore the oneness we were created to desire is through milestones and achievements. We have visions for our marriages, and we think that as we accomplish certain things, we will experience the intimacy that we know is missing. Couples think:

- When we make more money, then our marriage will be better.
- If we can just get out of debt, then we won't feel as much pressure, and our marriage will be better.
- When I get that promotion, it will be a game changer for us.
- When we buy that new house, it will make a lot of problems go away.
- If we could just have kids, that would bring us closer together.
- If we can just make it to our next anniversary, then I'll have hope for our marriage.

We create these if-then scenarios. If we could just have this or do that or accomplish this or build that or buy this or achieve that, *then* our marriages would finally be what we want them to be.

The problem is that none of these milestones or achievements brings the oneness we desire. There will always be another milestone. There will always be another achievement. When we look to an accomplishment or a stage of life to provide us with marital intimacy, we will always come back to ordinary.

New Expectations

This last attempt at oneness is why so many marriages become ordinary. When we realize that we can't change our spouses and we grasp that our milestones and achievements haven't brought us the fulfillment we thought they would, we create new expectations for our marriages.

In other words, we *settle*.

We settle for a smaller vision. We resign ourselves to the idea that this is the best our marriage can be. We lower our expectations. We stop dreaming about the future. We give in to the reality that this is the best version of oneness that we can create. Our new expectations lead us to a more isolated marriage that is more about coexisting than thriving. Intimacy is reduced to how many times a month we have sex rather than being fully known to our spouses. We come to believe that being fully known in our marriages isn't possible. Once upon a time we experienced intimacy and oneness in an extraordinary marriage; now we think of those days as a fairy tale.

ACHIEVING ONENESS

Oneness in marriage is possible. It isn't easy, but it is possible. And it only comes as each spouse individually pursues God.

When you decide to stop trying to change your spouse and pursue God instead, and when your spouse decides to not measure the health of your marriage through milestones and achievements but rather pursues God, the distance in your marriage decreases. Pursuing God looks different for everyone, because all of us are in different places in our relationships with God, but there are two things that will be true for each of us who longs to pursue God. First, we will choose to think about God. This involves personal prayer, reading God's Word, and becoming aware of God's promptings and presence. Second, pursuing God involves a willingness to surrender our rights and our desires to God for his desires and his plan. It is an invitation to allow him to change us.

Individually, as you move closer to God, then you naturally move closer to each other. It's a pursuit in which the ordinary dies and the extraordinary begins to live.

If we would spend the same amount of time and energy asking God to change ourselves as we do asking him to change our spouses, our marriages would be anything but ordinary. It is so easy for us to apply truth to our spouses before we apply it to ourselves. It is easy for us to see the faults in them and to stay blind to the faults that live in us. Oneness in our marriages is restored as we ask—and *allow*—God to change us. Even if your spouse doesn't change, your marriage will be better because *you* will be changed.

A question we are often asked is, What if my spouse isn't pursuing God at the same pace as I am? What we have come to realize is that all of our journeys will look different. Your pursuit of God doesn't have to be at the same pace, just with the same commitment. Each of us will go through peaks and valleys in our relationship with God. It is our commitment to that journey that allows us to experience oneness the way God intended.

A BATTLE PLAN

One of the things we have learned is that there is a huge difference between good intentions and being intentional. We said in the last chapter that most marriages don't intend to drift into ordinary. Ordinary is the by-product of the equation time + unintentionality = ordinary.

In order to move beyond ordinary, we have to be intentional. We have an enemy who is intentionally coming against our marriage relationships. We won't drift into extraordinary; we will have to fight for it.

Intentionality + time = extraordinary. Here are two crucial ways you can fight the battle for an extraordinary marriage.

Pray for Your Spouse

As a pastor, I (Justin) get paid to pray. Trisha and I have always believed in the power of prayer. We knew the importance of prayer. We prayed all the time. We would pray for small-group leaders. We would pray for people having marital problems. We would pray for people who came up after the Sunday service and wanted to rededicate their lives to Christ. We just never prayed for each other.

Looking back, I know how ridiculous this seems. How could we not pray for each other? I would pray for Trisha occasionally. It would go something like this: "Dear God, please prompt Trisha to not gripe at me when I get home tonight. In Jesus' name, amen." I didn't consistently pray for Trisha and her needs, desires, and feelings. I never took time to lift her up to God as I should have.

If you want to change the climate of your marriage immediately, start praying for your spouse. Then you will realize that you are engaging the spiritual battle in your marriage rather than becoming a victim of it.

Pray with Your Spouse

I read a statistic not long ago that shocked me: less than 8 percent of Christian couples say that they pray together on a regular basis. While that is shocking, it isn't surprising. For some reason it is difficult to pray with your spouse.

Praying with your spouse is huge in fighting for his or her heart. This may feel weird at first and may not feel natural. There isn't anything more intimate—*including sex*—than praying with your spouse and hearing your spouse pray for you. Our prayers to God are some of the most intimate conversations we have. We share our hopes, our dreams, our fears, our insecurities, our failures, and our successes with our heavenly Father.

When I pray with Trisha, I am allowed to hear her articulate the things in her life that are most precious to her. I am able to understand her more. I am invited into a part of her heart that is sacred. There is a bond and a connection that is formed through praying together that can't be simulated or created in any other way. The Holy Spirit joins us and draws us closer together as we seek God with our spouses. This aspect alone has been a huge part of our journey, and we have heard so many stories from other couples who have chosen to share this part of their heart with their spouses and have experienced intimacy in ways they never thought possible.

Marriage is no ordinary battle. To overcome an ordinary marriage, you have to fight *for* your spouse, not *with* your spouse.

QUESTIONS

1. Can you recall the very first argument in your marriage? If so, what was it about?

2. Can you remember a "Did God really say . . ." moment that altered the way you looked at your life and your marriage? Why was this moment so influential?

3. As a couple, do you live with an awareness that there is a spiritual battle for your marriage? How do you respond to that battle?

4. Do you feel comfortable praying with your spouse? Why or why not? Would you consider praying with your spouse for the next 30 days?

3.

NO ORDINARY HONESTY

WHAT PREVENTS us from being fully known?

The greatest adversary to being fully known is dishonesty. And fear is the driving force in most of our dishonesty. Our fears are often greater than our desire for intimacy and leave our marriages ordinary.

Those who compromise honesty generally do so because of three fears: fear of being exposed, fear of emotional pain, and fear of not being loved. When any of these fears is larger than our desire for intimacy, ordinary becomes the norm in our marriages.

Many of us have something in our lives that we hope no one finds out. Many of us live with secrets that even our spouses don't know. Maybe it's the number of people we slept with before marriage. Maybe it's an eating disorder we had or currently struggle with. Maybe it's lustful thoughts about a coworker. Maybe it's a pornography addiction. Maybe it's abuse we suffered as children.

Our secrets don't always have to be something we've done;

often they are something that was done to us. But our fear is that someone will expose our secrets. That fear—fear of being exposed—feeds the fear of emotional pain.

We don't want to be exposed, because we've calculated the emotional pain our secrets or our lies or our addictions or our confessions will cause, and we have concluded that the emotional pain we will endure or the emotional pain we will cause will be greater than any good that could come from being exposed. So we continue to hide. We continue to pretend that things are better than they really are, thinking we are sparing ourselves and those we love from emotional pain. That fear is fueled by another fear.

We are convinced that if we were exposed and our secret was found out, the emotional pain it would cause would make us unlovable. So we think, *If my wife ever knew that about me, she would stop loving me.* Or, *If my husband found out about that, he would be done with me.* Or, *If I am honest about that, I will be all alone.* Our dishonesty, we believe, will help our marriages, not hurt them.

We've talked a lot in the first two chapters about oneness. Oneness can seem like an abstract concept—how do we quantify *oneness*? Oneness—as we will repeat throughout this book—is intimacy, being fully known. All of us desire to know and be fully known by someone. We all desire to experience intimacy with God and intimacy with another human being. God gave us that desire, and it is God's design for marriage.

But while there is this deep desire for intimacy, there is another part of us that is fearful of someone really knowing us, really seeing the dark parts of our hearts. We have a desire to be known, but a competing desire to avoid pain. We want to be emotionally safe. The problem is that biblical intimacy isn't safe.

TRISHA:

One evening when Micah was just a baby, I could not get him to stop crying. He was a colicky baby to begin with, but this particular day, his tears of unhappiness seemed inconsolable. He had cried all day, and by the evening I was worn out. Unfortunately, Justin had a meeting that night and couldn't come home to help. But a few hours into the evening, I was losing my mind and begged Justin to come home. Justin left his meeting to take care of us. What I didn't know was what had transpired along the way.

The only thing that seemed to calm Micah was the shower. I would stand in the shower with him and let the warm water soothe his pain. By eight o'clock, I just stayed in my bathrobe rather than getting dressed, knowing that another shower was just around the corner. Relieved Justin was on his way home, I sat on the couch and released a deep sigh because help was coming.

But my help came sooner than expected, and I was startled by the sound of our doorbell.

Listening to the doorbell frantically ring, I thought, *Justin was twenty minutes away. How did he get here so quickly, and why is he ringing our doorbell?* When I opened the door, there stood two male EMS workers with their ambulance lights ablaze in the background. Sleep deprived and exhausted, I assumed they had the wrong apartment. But the younger of the two said, "Are you Trisha Davis?"

"Um . . . yes?" I replied.

Can I just pause here before I finish this story? I need to say that I am a rules follower; Justin is not.

While Justin made a mad rush home to his crying son and crazy wife, a police officer pulled him over for speeding. In order to get out of the ticket, he told the officer that there was an emergency at home. The officer said he had to call an ambulance in order to let Justin out of the ticket.

And so there I sat, half-dressed, hair and face a mess, trying to follow the rules and tell them there was no emergency—just a crying baby and a soon-to-be-crying husband!

To my amazement, the older EMT showed me grace and dealt with my "emergency." He took Micah from my arms, gently rocked him, and in minutes handed back to me a miracle—a sleeping baby.

Looking back, I can see that this was just the first of many instances when I went from being enchanted by the way Justin would attempt to fix my problems to *expecting* him to fix all my problems. It was really funny at the time that Justin told the police officer there was an emergency in order to escape a ticket. Little did I know that compromising truth to escape consequences would become a pattern for Justin and for our marriage for years to come. Distorting truth and compromising truth often seems innocent and harmless, but it always comes with a price. The price for us would be eroded intimacy and broken trust.

JUSTIN:

One of the complicating factors during the time of Trisha's parents' divorce was my job situation. I was becoming increasingly unhappy as our student ministry outgrew the desire the church had to reach kids who were far from God. There was constant tension between the elders and me because our student ministry was growing at a pace they weren't comfortable with.

I brought that tension home. I wanted to go to a bigger, more progressive church, a church that would embrace a growing student ministry. Our home situation seemed like a perfect storm: I was unhappy with my job; Trisha longed to be closer to her family. I wanted to pretend that we didn't argue all the time. I wanted to pretend that we felt confident as parents. I wanted to make believe that Trisha wasn't emotionally needy and I wasn't emotionally disconnected. I wanted to pretend that our marriage wasn't as weary and frayed as it already was. I wanted to pretend that things were okay with us even when they weren't. Because I am a fixer, I thought that if we could move closer to her family, that would solve everything. We could find a bigger, better ministry so I would be happy, and we could move closer to Trisha's family so she could be happy.

I made some phone calls to pastors, professors, and other contacts I had in the Chicagoland area, seeking a youth ministry position closer to Trisha's home. A little over a year into our first student ministry, I resigned, and we moved to Batavia, Illinois, to a bigger church and student ministry.

But far from fixing our problems, the move made some of them more evident than ever. One of them, as Trisha mentioned, was my not always being truthful. I remember the first time I intentionally distorted truth with Trisha. We had been in Illinois only a few months when we took a group of students to a campus event at Lincoln Christian College. The college was just a few hours away, so we loaded up a few fifteen-passenger vans and headed south. I thought this would be a great way for us to get to know the students and to build the foundation for a healthy student ministry.

The kickoff to the weekend was a concert performed by Audio Adrenaline, one of my favorite Christian bands at the time. Because Trisha and I were only a little more than a year removed from being students at the college, we still had several friends who were there, and I was asked to help with security at the concert. I was all in favor of that, because I tend to be starstruck, and working security would give me an all-access pass to stalk—I mean, *meet*—the band. I was pumped.

My security responsibility during the concert was pretty easy. I had to stand at the front of the auditorium and make sure none of the kids tried to get on stage. Trisha and I stood next to each other during the concert, and our students were allowed to be up in the front as well. It seemed like a win for everyone.

About halfway through the concert, my eyes caught Trisha's, and she looked furious. She said, "I can't believe you!" and left the auditorium. I knew in my heart what she meant, and I followed her outside, through the lobby, and into the parking lot. She was walking fast, crying hard, and not interested in anything I had to say. I repeatedly asked her what was wrong. She turned and looked at me dead in the eyes, tears streaming down her face, and said, "I saw you checking out that girl in front of you. You were staring at her body!"

She was right, of course, but there was no way I was going to admit it. I had to convince her she was wrong. I was defensive. I acted appalled. I pretended she was crazy. I matched the intensity of her accusation with determination to prove my innocence. I told her I would never do that. I told her she was projecting her parents' divorce on me and that this was about her insecurity and not my lusting. I broke her down, convincing her that our marriage was different; I was different; she didn't have to feel insecure or anxious. What was going to destroy our marriage was her living with a posture of accusation, not my lusting after other women. What I've just said in a few sentences took a few hours of manipulation then.

The three fears mentioned at the beginning of the chapter will do incredible things. Fear of being found out, fear of emotional pain, and fear of not being loved convinced me that the lies I was telling were helping our marriage, while I was actually tearing Trisha apart—I just couldn't see it at the time. My intention wasn't to hurt Trisha; it was to protect our marriage—and me. I know that sounds crazy given the blatant lies I told her, but in my mind, I was terrified that if she knew the truth about me, our marriage would be over. If I told her the truth, she wouldn't love me anymore. I thought our marriage was too delicate to survive my admitting to her that I *was* lusting; I *was* staring; I *was* checking that girl out. There was no way that confession would be good for our marriage, so I simply distorted the truth. Hiding truth, I felt, would have fewer consequences than admitting truth.

TRISHA:

Much like Lucy in The Chronicles of Narnia, I'd somehow stumbled through a wardrobe to an unfamiliar land. But the world I had stumbled into wasn't filled with strange people and animals, but rather familiar people doing strange things. I grew up knowing friends whose parents had divorced, but *my* parents were different.

And I had friends whose husbands were caught lusting after other women, but *my* husband was different.

My parents' divorce opened my eyes. I realized that things were not at all as they seemed. If I had known where the wardrobe door was to go back to the way things were, I would have run full speed back through it. Catching Justin looking at that girl confirmed that he was no different from the other untrustworthy men I knew. Justin had now become part of this new and unfamiliar landscape.

As Justin chased me in the bitter cold across the frozen field, I felt disoriented. My heart was beating fast, causing my body to feel like it was on fire, matching the anger blazing in my heart. I continued running across the field, thinking, *If my parents' marriage crashed after twenty-five years, what will keep ours from falling apart after only two?*

Justin kept calling after me, "Trisha, stop!" I didn't care who might have been watching or listening; I just wanted to leave. But I eventually did stop and screamed through my violent tears, "You told me you were different! You told me you didn't struggle with lust, but you lied! I saw you undressing her with your eyes! And you know what? You can have her, because I don't care anymore!"

Justin tried to explain that what I saw didn't happen. He told me I was projecting the hurt my dad caused me onto him. But I knew what I saw.

Still, the more Justin talked, the more I was convinced that he was right and this was my issue, not his. I was defeated.

I didn't know it, but a piece of my heart grew as cold as the field I was standing on. I was resigned to the possibility that this new world was where I now lived. No longer would I allow my heart to love Justin intimately. Rather, I would hold him at arm's length.

JUSTIN & TRISHA:

When we act out of fear, we gradually drift into two types of dishonesty: distortion of truth and withholding truth. Distorting the truth is intentionally and consciously lying. The word *distortion* implies deliberately giving misleading or false information. Withholding truth is different from distorting the truth because it isn't outright lying—it is not sharing all of the details. It is not offering truth when you have the opportunity. It is hiding information or emotions from someone.

We attempt to justify both forms of lying with a belief that we are protecting intimacy in our marriages, but the decisions we make to compromise honesty gradually destroy intimacy, a little at a time. We don't set out to lie to our spouses. We don't intend to be dishonest. But ordinary marriages live in the gray area of partial honesty.

DAVID & BATHSHEBA: TRUTH DISTORTED

In the story of King David, we see a man who experiences great intimacy with God. God anoints him. He is set apart to be the king of Israel and a spiritual exemplar to God's people. He knows God's heart, and God knows his. From David's youth as a giant-slaying shepherd boy to his inauguration as king over all Israel, God is with him.

One afternoon David is on the roof of his palace, and he sees a woman bathing. Captivated by her beauty, he sends one of his messengers to find out more about this woman. His messenger returns to explain that she is the wife of Uriah, a faithful soldier in the Israelite army, who is away at war fighting for David.

At this moment, David would have known exactly who Bathsheba was. In 1 Chronicles 11, Uriah the Hittite is listed as one of David's mighty warriors. Uriah was one of thirty men who had fought with and for David in the most epic of battles. Uriah would have been very close—in proximity if not regular comradery—to David.

But even with this new information, David overlooks what Uriah has done for him and makes a really poor decision. It is a story you are probably familiar with: David sends for Bathsheba and sleeps with her. *No one will know*, he thinks. He is the king and has the power to keep things quiet. But sin has a way of revealing itself, even when we think we can hide it. A short time later, Bathsheba realizes she is pregnant.

Much like Justin on that cold winter's night, David decides to continue lying rather than tell the truth. David calls Uriah back from the front, invites him to the palace, and then sends him home to sleep with his wife so David can cover up his part in Bathsheba's pregnancy. But Uriah is so loyal to the king that he refuses to go home. The next day, David invites Uriah back to the palace to convince him to go home and sleep with his wife, even getting him drunk, but again Uriah refuses out of loyalty to David and his fellow soldiers. David then escalates his cover-up scheme, and he has Uriah put on the front lines of the battle and killed.

Like David, I (Trisha) for years felt that even though my family had to endure a lot of tough and heartbreaking battles, God was with me. Like David, when times got hard, I would turn to God, and God would answer. But as David's circumstances started to change, so did he. When David committed adultery, he not only covered up what he did from those around him, but even worse, he hid from God. Just like Adam and Eve in the Garden, David attempted to deal with sin by hiding it. Justin and I were no different.

Unconfessed sin leads to either distorting the truth or withholding it. Both erode intimacy and break trust.

ICEBERGS & WATER LEVELS: WITHHOLDING TRUTH

There is another type of dishonesty that keeps our marriages ordinary. This kind of dishonesty is more subtle. It seems less damaging. It doesn't feel like such a big deal. It isn't distorting the truth; it is simply withholding the truth.

Let's pretend that our lives are icebergs. Our family relationships, our friendships, our work and school relationships, our marriages, and our relationships with God all make up this iceberg.

What's dangerous about icebergs is that what lies below the surface is usually larger than what can be seen above the waterline. The part of an iceberg that isn't visible is the part that has the potential to do the most damage. I think the same thing is true in our lives. Each relational level of our lives is like a waterline, and as we allow that waterline to lower in our relationships, more of who we are is exposed—to others and to God.

Unlike icebergs, the waterline in our lives is totally within our control. It is totally up to us how high or low that waterline is. How low we allow the waterline to go will determine the intimacy we are capable of experiencing in our relationships and in our marriages.

The first waterline in our lives we might call "image." The image waterline is the level we work hard to make appealing. This waterline leaves the part of the iceberg above the surface that everyone sees. It represents the most visible and public parts of your life. This is your job. This is the car you drive. This is the house you live in. This is the smile you put on your face on the way to church. This is what your golfing buddies think about you. This is the school you want your kids to go to. This is the neighborhood you aspire to live in. This is the public persona you display for those you want to impress. This is what your neighbors think about you. This is the area of your life that you try really hard to make respectable and noticeable. This is what you allow the majority of your relationships to know about you. This is the surface level of our lives.

There is a second waterline in most of our lives, the relationship waterline. This waterline represents what your friends know about you. When you allow others to see your life at this waterline, more of your heart is exposed. This waterline is reserved for a select group of people in your life. It allows a smaller group of people to know more about you. They know your successes as well as your failures. They know your dreams and your hopes. At this waterline, you share your story and go beyond the exterior you've cultivated. The smaller group at this waterline is allowed to see your dysfunctions and weaknesses. This is where your relationship with your spouse likely started.

The waterline probably started high when you were dating. Your spouse could do no wrong. She was perfect, you never fought, he didn't know your past, she didn't know your flaws. But then there was a shift, and you realized that you could trust this person. You could be more vulnerable with him or her. You could share more of yourself. As your relationship grew, you made a conscious decision to allow the person you were dating to become the person you would marry. You lowered the waterline; you exposed more of your heart.

The next waterline is marriage. This is the waterline reserved for your spouse. It is the most intimidating waterline and leaves your heart exposed and vulnerable. You envisioned your spouse knowing everything about you and you knowing everything about your spouse. This is the part of your heart that you allow only your spouse to see.

When you stood at the altar and said, "I do," you didn't anticipate there being another waterline. In that moment, you probably believed that in your marriage relationship you would have the safety and security to be fully known, to be fully exposed, to have no part of your life below the waterline. That was God's vision for your marriage, and it was likely your vision as well.

But the longer we are married, the easier it is to allow the waterline of our hearts to creep back up and leave more and more of our hearts below the surface, not visible even to our spouses.

There is another waterline in most of our lives. It is what we call "hiddenness," and this is the part of our hearts that we don't allow even our spouses to see. This is the part of our hearts where we withhold truth. This is that part of our hearts where we say,

"I could never tell my husband that."

"If my wife ever knew that about me, it would be over."

"I don't need to share that with my husband; it's not that big of a deal."

"What my wife doesn't know won't hurt her."

This was the lustful part of my (Justin's) heart. This was the part of my heart that I knew was there but didn't think I could share with Trisha. It was the hidden part of me.

What we realize in our marriages is that we do want to spend the rest of our lives with the other person, but we don't want to share all of our hearts. This last level is the waterline that costs us something. As our willingness to share this part of our hearts increases, our vulnerability to risk and hurt also increases.

For most of us, we get to a place where we not only think we can hide this part of our hearts from our spouses, but we think we can hide it from God, too. If we can go to church enough, if we can be spiritual enough, if we can read our Bibles enough, if we can be good enough, then maybe God won't notice the parts of our hearts we have yet to expose to him.

Maybe the ordinary state of our marriages has less to do with the marriage and more to do with the truth we withhold or distort in our relationships with God. When we hide truth, we limit the level of intimacy we are capable of experiencing in that relationship. We put a cap on being fully known. Partial truth will never lead to complete intimacy. Partial truth always leads to ordinary relationships, with God and with our spouses. And we can never have extraordinary relationships with our spouses when we are settling for an ordinary relationship with God.

Intimacy, being fully known, is built upon a foundation of truth telling.

LIVING WITH NO SECRETS

It is easy to think that the solution to our dishonesty is simply, "Just tell the truth." But it's not that easy. If it were that easy, we would all be great truth tellers. Intimacy comes with a price, and the cost of intimacy is complete honesty. Complete honesty with God, complete honesty with ourselves, complete honesty with our spouses. The problem that most of us have is that we think we can *behave* our way into being honest. Being honest isn't a condition of our behavior; it is a condition of our hearts. If we want our lying to change, we have to allow God to change our hearts.

I (Justin) have struggled with honesty my entire life. I have distorted, exaggerated, and withheld truth in ways that have caused immense damage to those I love the most. More than that, my dishonesty has broken intimacy in my relationship with God. Because truth telling is a prerequisite to intimacy, it has become a nonnegotiable in my life. Here are some questions I ask myself that allow God the space in my heart he needs to transform me:

1. Is the fear of the consequences of the truth greater than my commitment to tell the truth?

2. Am I telling myself the truth?

3. Is there a truth I have distorted or am distorting right now?

4. Is there something I have withheld or am currently withholding from my spouse?

Let's go back to the story of David. He has already committed adultery and murder. The king of Israel—in no uncertain terms—has sinned. Not only has he sinned, he has hidden his sin and withheld truth. For almost an entire year, this sin goes unconfessed. God has had enough, and he wants to confront David.

In 2 Samuel 12, we read how God sends the prophet Nathan to confront David's sin, to lower the waterline of his heart and expose the iceberg he's been hiding:

> So the LORD sent Nathan the prophet to tell David this
> story: "There were two men in a certain town. One was
> rich, and one was poor. The rich man owned a great
> many sheep and cattle. The poor man owned nothing but
> one little lamb he had bought. He raised that little lamb,
> and it grew up with his children. It ate from the man's
> own plate and drank from his cup. He cuddled it in his

arms like a baby daughter. One day a guest arrived at the home of the rich man. But instead of killing an animal from his own flock or herd, he took the poor man's lamb and killed it and prepared it for his guest."

David was furious. "As surely as the LORD lives," he vowed, "any man who would do such a thing deserves to die! He must repay four lambs to the poor man for the one he stole and for having no pity."

Then Nathan said to David, "You are that man!"

2 SAMUEL 12:1-7

This is what I love about the story of David: with those four words—"You are that man!"—the waterline of David's heart is lowered and his entire life is exposed. Most of the time, like David, we also wait until we are exposed before we realize the tremendous freedom of living with no secrets. David is exposed, and in the process of being exposed, he realizes the power of confession.

Look what David says in Psalm 32:

Blessed is the one
    whose transgressions are forgiven,
    whose sins are covered.
Blessed is the one
    whose sin the LORD does not count
        against them
    and in whose spirit is no deceit.

When I kept silent,
    my bones wasted away
    through my groaning all day long.
For day and night
    your hand was heavy on me;
my strength was sapped
    as in the heat of summer.

Then I acknowledged my sin to you
    and did not cover up my iniquity.
I said, "I will confess
    my transgressions to the LORD."
And you forgave
    the guilt of my sin.

Therefore let all the faithful pray to you
    while you may be found;
surely the rising of the mighty waters
    will not reach them.
You are my hiding place;
    you will protect me from trouble
    and surround me with songs
        of deliverance.
PSALM 32:1-7, NIV

Maybe you are in a place similar to the one David was in. You are wasting away because you are silent about your sin. You have secrets and mistakes and things you have convinced yourself that you can never tell your spouse. You are tired. Your marriage is tired.

Maybe as you read this chapter you know that you are David: you have withheld truth for a long time, and it has put distance between you and God and you and your spouse. Your marriage is ordinary, and it may be because your relationship is built on only partial honesty. You want to tell the truth, but you know it will hurt.

I read a Tweet from Andy Stanley that said, "We fear the consequences of confession because we have yet to realize the consequences of concealment." This certainly seems true from my vantage point. The consequences of your concealment may be less visible than the consequences of your confession, but they will always do more damage.

The path to extraordinary is confession, but how do you choose confession?

May I offer a few suggestions? Trisha and I have benefited from the help and guidance of a Christian marriage counselor. We highly recommend that couples who struggle in the area of honesty work with a marriage counselor to help refine and improve their marriages. Especially if you have truth that has been withheld or distorted for a long time, the expertise of a marriage counselor can be essential to help you and your spouse start the healing process. Confession doesn't do any good if it doesn't lead to transformation. A counselor will help you move toward transformation.

Second, be patient in this process. The odds are that it took you some time to drift into ordinary; it will take you some time to arrive at extraordinary. There will be pain. Unlike the pain you are in now, the pain of truth telling is redemptive pain. It is like the setting of a broken bone. It does hurt in that moment, but the result is a bone put into a place to heal, strong and whole. That is what you will experience in this process. As you allow the waterline of your heart and life to be lowered, it will be painful. You may have to deal with truth you have been avoiding for a long time. But it will be worth it.

I love what David says in verse seven of Psalm 32: "You are my hiding place." Life is lived differently when we stop trying to hide our sin and instead allow God himself to be our hiding place. When God is our hiding place, we don't have to run from him; we run *to* him because he is our refuge. Hiding in God means he knows all of us. We share our fears; we share our sorrows; we share our failures; we share our past; we share our hearts. Hiding in God means that everything is exposed before him and that what people see most when they look at us is him.

When God is your hiding place, you don't have to distort truth. When God is your hiding place, you don't have to pretend. When God is your hiding place, ordinary makes way for extraordinary.

Ordinary marriages share part of the truth and put a lid on intimacy. Extraordinary marriages live with no secrets.

QUESTIONS

1. Of the three fears listed, which do you struggle with the most: fear of being exposed, fear of emotional pain, or fear of not being loved? Why do you think you struggle with this?

2. Being fully known is a choice to lower the waterline. What are the icebergs in your marriage that need to rise to the surface?

3. What does the story of King David reveal about unconfessed sin and withholding or distorting truth? About lowered waterlines and repentance? In what ways do you see yourself or your marriage in David's story?

4. What are some ways you need to rely on God to give you the marriage you've always wanted?

4.

NO ORDINARY JOURNEY

IN EXODUS 15, the extraordinary journey God has taken Moses and the people of Israel on takes its own turn of unexpected events. If God is powerful enough to do so many miracles, it seems reasonable to conclude that he will also be good with directions. But only *three days* into their journey, the Israelites start to lose faith. Only three days after singing God's praises (see Exodus 15:1-24), the complaints start flying.

How quickly Moses moves from hero to villain in their eyes! With great intensity and speed, the people of Israel voice their unmet expectations: "This is all Moses' fault! We should never have moved."

Have you ever taken a huge leap of faith only to find that you may have romanticized the outcome? What you pictured in your mind was this extraordinary journey that would somehow make life feel better or more complete. Maybe your first leap of faith was getting a college degree, buying a new house, starting a business, or marrying your spouse.

Maybe your romanticized journey started in a childhood that never became the fairy tale you imagined it would be, and like me (Trisha), you entered into your marriage expecting life to be different. Because your spouse was different, you would be different, and therefore life would be different. Weeks, months, or years into your marriage, your unmet expectations feel like the same desert in which you started.

If you've made it this far in the book, then you know that just hours into our epic adventure of marriage, we found out that our fairy-tale story wasn't going quite the way we had planned.

In our attempts to dream big, we made sure to create lists of expectations for how our dreams should become realities. But when those expectations weren't met, frustration set in and dreams died as life moved into the ordinary.

TRISHA:

When we made our leap of faith to move back to the Chicagoland area, we needed temporary housing until our apartment was ready. We found refuge with the Trethaways, whose son Chris attended Bible college with us. Their house was a spacious open concept with windows from floor to ceiling. (This is an important detail to remember.)

Only a day after arriving, Justin left to begin his first day as a youth pastor at our new church. Our then-one-year-old son, Micah, had free rein of the house. Just an hour into our day together, I used the restroom on the main level, and after I flushed the toilet, it overflowed onto Mrs. Trethaway's beautiful bathroom mats and floor. A bit frustrated, I put Micah into his high chair so I could clean up the mess. *It's going to be okay*, I told myself.

As the bath mats washed, I let Micah out to play. Things were looking up. After all, I was "back home," closer to family, which meant life and ministry would be easier. After putting the mats in the dryer, I walked into the kitchen, only to realize my toddler had gone MIA! I could hear him crying but couldn't find him. I was freaking out. A minute felt like an hour as I desperately tried to draw myself closer to his cries. Out of the corner of my eye I noticed that one of the windows was open and the screen was missing. Missing toddler, missing screen could only mean one thing. Yes, Micah had fallen *out the window* and onto (or rather into) a bush.

His big brown eyes looked as relieved as mine when I scooped him up and held him tight. Quietly saying to myself, *It's going to be okay*, I decided that spending the rest of the day in our bedroom with a locked door and closed window would make for a safer afternoon. Before we locked ourselves away, one more trip to the bathroom was needed, and this time, to play it safe, I used the upstairs bathroom *and* took Micah with me. Minutes later—you guessed right—toilet number two was now wildly overflowing, and this time mats *and* a toddler were soaked in gross toilet water. There was no *It's going to be okay* talk at this point, only a loud shout of "This sucks!"

Long before text messages, communication was a simple phone call. In the midst of the chaos, Justin called to check in, expecting a simple "Things are going great" to flow from my mouth. Instead he received a play-by-play of my day. Before I could get to the part about Micah's going MIA, Justin interrupted and said he was sorry, but he had to go—the staff was taking him out to lunch. *Well, how wonderful for him*, I thought later as I ate my cold pieces of cut-up hot dog left over from Micah's lunch.

After two overflowed toilets, an MIA toddler, and an uncaring husband, a nap sounded like the best way to retreat. I was overwhelmed with frustration. I felt like *I* was the one packing and unpacking again. *I* was the one figuring out where to go grocery shopping. *I* was the one who had to find new doctors and get records transferred. In my mind, *I* was pulling most of the weight on the home front while Justin "worked" at lunches where he was served and didn't have to eat cold food from a screaming toddler's plate.

As I lay in bed trying not to make a peep, hoping that Micah would fall asleep in his portable crib, the same darkness that had overtaken the room took over my heart. I had romanticized this move as being to the Promised Land, giving me the extraordinary marriage and ministry I longed for. This move would fix so much in my life and my relationship with Justin. But just like the Israelites, days into this new journey the only thing that had changed was the landscape. I was no closer to living an extraordinary marriage than I was before, and all I could think was, *We should never have moved.*

JUSTIN:

One of the misconceptions I had in ministry was my own importance. I am a very driven, goal-oriented person. I had been cut from the basketball team in seventh grade and was cut again in eighth grade. What would have defeated some challenged me. I left the locker room in eighth grade telling myself that no one would ever tell me I wasn't good enough again. I wanted to prove how valuable I was, and basketball became my way to do that.

I had the same conquest and achievement mind-set in my relationship with Trisha. She didn't want to go out with me—I wasn't good enough. I wanted to prove to her that I was worth dating. I wanted to fulfill her every need. I wanted her to be completely satisfied in our relationship. I didn't want her to feel discontented in any way. I found my value in being strong when she was weak. I found my value in solving problems and coming to her rescue. That is what a good husband does, I thought, and I wanted to exceed her expectations.

Now eighteen months into marriage, that desire to exceed expectations moved from marriage to ministry. My desire to impress others, to be valuable to others and feel important, drove me.

A few months after we arrived in Illinois, I was asked to speak at our new church on Sunday morning. The senior pastor was going out of town, and he wanted to give me the chance to speak and to allow the congregation to get to know me. I was honored and excited. I don't remember what the message was about, but I do remember the response after the service—and how the response made me feel.

I was standing in the lobby after the service, and an older man approached me with his hand outstretched. "I've been coming to this church for over fifteen years," he said, "and that was the best message I've ever heard on a Sunday morning." I smiled, said thank you, and told him how much I appreciated his kindness.

A short time later, I was asked to speak again. I felt so much pressure. How could I impress these people again? How could I top my last message? How could I get as many compliments after this message as I had after my last one?

The week I was speaking arrived, and I had nothing. No great idea. No inspired word. What I did have was a stack of John Ortberg tapes in my car. John Ortberg was a teaching pastor at Willow Creek at the time and one of my favorite teachers. I went to my car and grabbed a tape. For the next two hours, I sat in my office and transcribed one of his messages word for word. A few days later, I stood on the stage and delivered John Ortberg's message as if it were my own.

Subtly and slowly, I began to rely more on what *I* did in ministry than on what God could do. I suffered from the messiah complex. I wanted to be everyone's savior, and my ministry and my marriage became completely dependent on me and my performance.

My performance was an indicator of my value. Without even realizing it, I thought, *If I'm not at this event, then it won't be as successful. If I don't speak this weekend, then students won't come back next week. If we don't get together with this couple, then their marriage will fail. If we don't have them over for dinner, then they'll stop serving.*

While I suffered from the messiah complex, Trisha, it seemed, suffered from the "reverse messiah complex," a state of mind in which a husband or wife places godlike or messiah-sized expectations on his or her spouse. When Trisha experienced loneliness, anxiety, stress, fear, depression, insecurity, or uncertainty, she'd look to me to fill her needs. And because of my messiah complex,

I looked to solve those things in her. But what this led to was an accumulation of unmet expectations.

TRISHA:

In the movie *Groundhog Day*, the main character relives the same day over and over again. This is how our marriage began to feel. Six months into our time at our new church, the youth ministry had spread like wildfire, and not only did the students love our style, but their parents did as well.

But it was like we had only hit the snooze button on the year before, and now we were waking up to the same situation. Conflict arose between Justin and the senior pastor at the church. Justin was young and driven and didn't mind pushing the boundaries. He was an "ask for forgiveness, not permission" type of leader. The senior pastor had been at the church for ten years and had settled into a comfortable pace of ministry. He received Justin's ideas as a threat to his leadership.

I don't think Justin intended to challenge our pastor's authority—at first. But the defensive response Justin received altered his motives, and he did start questioning our pastor's leadership and desire to see the church grow. When Justin realized that things at the church were not likely to change, his response was to look for another opportunity. He talked about needing to move again, but this time I was not enthusiastic about the change. I knew that another ministry wouldn't bring us to the Promised Land—just another desert.

One thing we *were* on the same page about was trying for baby number two. Since Micah had been a surprise, it was fun to "try" for the second baby, and it kept my mind from fully engaging with the possibility that we could be moving again.

Unbeknownst to Justin, we got pregnant on our first try. Because Justin's birthday was just a week away, I thought this would be an epic birthday present to give him. With some close friends at my side, I rented a limo and surprised Justin at the church. I expected him to be stoked to find out that we were going into the city in style and that he was being lavished with such love . . . but he wasn't. When we shouted, "Surprise!" the only thing he could say was, "Where did you get the money to do such a thing!" Strike number one!

I thought it best to give him his gift in the limo to break the awkwardness of his reaction to my first surprise. I reached into my purse, grabbed a bulky envelope, and handed it to Justin. My girlfriends and I were so giddy, we could hardly contain ourselves. Justin, still puzzled by the whole experience, took the envelope, opened it, and pulled out a positive pregnancy test and a card that said, "We are having a baby!"

I had imagined that Justin would well up with tears, embrace me, and whisper sweetly into my ear, "God is so amazing. . . ." Instead, I received a "What you talkin' about, Willis?" look. He looked upset, as if I had gotten pregnant so soon just to make his life difficult. If my girlfriends could shoot fire from their eyes, I'm certain Justin would have become toast that day. Strike number two!

Six months later, six months pregnant, we moved—again. By this point in our marriage, *moving* had become a four-letter word. Six moves and four ministries (including our part-time ministries in college) in twenty-eight months was our current record at this point. Each move seemed to have some rhyme or reason, so, I reasoned, what would one more move hurt—especially knowing that this time we were moving to a house! A house with a backyard, sidewalks, and beautiful, large trees.

Although the house was a great cover-up to eventually convince myself that *this* move could be the Promised Land, I slowly drifted into a mind-set that conditions and expectations needed to be met in order for me to move forward in anything. If Justin wanted me to move, then he needed to move me to something better. If he wanted me to be involved in his ministry, he needed to find a babysitter and the money to make it happen. I became an expert in keeping score. No longer was I dreaming limos, babies, and partnership for our relationship. Rather, if-then statements became my guide. They were my new way of communication. Countless instances of Justin's not doing "this" so I could respond with "that" allowed our marriage not only to drift into ordinary but to stay camped out there.

JUSTIN & TRISHA:

EXTRAORDINARY JOURNEY, ORDINARY EXPECTATIONS

Reading through the life of Moses as recorded in Exodus, I (Trisha) am often dumbfounded by the epic step of faith God asks Moses to take to lead the Israelites out of Egypt. To get things started, God appears in a burning bush. *A. Burning. Bush.* I don't know about you, but if I saw a bush on fire and heard a voice calling from it, my first response would be to call 911 and then Google the nearest mental hospital! If there was ever a way to start an extraordinary journey, this was the way to go. But God doesn't stop with an awesome display of pyrotechnics. He continues his awesomeness by bringing plagues on Egypt, parting the Red Sea for the Israelites' escape, purifying bitter water, and making food rain down from the sky. This is an extraordinary journey!

When I allow my mind to envision the scene, I can't help but laugh and, honestly, become a bit self-righteous about how ridiculous Moses' response is. God shows up in an audacious way and clearly communicates the step of faith he's asking of Moses, but rather than embrace the call, Moses makes several attempts to protest it! Look at Exodus 4:13: "Lord, please! Send anyone else."

Seriously, Moses? God comes in the form of a bush *that's on fire but not burning up*, and you are arguing with him? Not only does Moses argue with God, but he has some expectations of how God's rescuing should all unfold. From his staff turning into a snake to Aaron's speaking on his behalf, Moses is willing to move only if God does what Moses expects him to do.

Maybe you're like me and read this with your mouth agape,

thinking, *There is no way I would have behaved like that.* But when I am honest with myself, I know that most likely, I would have demanded even more.

THE REVERSE MESSIAH COMPLEX

I (Justin) mentioned earlier that while I was suffering from a messiah complex—an inflated sense of my own importance—Trisha had the opposite problem, a reverse messiah complex. We earlier defined *reverse messiah complex* as "a state of mind in which a husband or wife places godlike or messiah-sized expectations on his or her spouse." While we're talking about expectations, let's unpack the reverse messiah complex a little more.

When we get married, we carry this invisible backpack down the aisle with us. That backpack is filled with dreams, desires, and wishes. It is full of the hopes and anticipations we have been building and accumulating our entire lives. The problem is that most of the time this invisible backpack becomes a heavy load of unmet expectations after the wedding. Many of us get married with an unspoken clause in our vows. We say, "I do," but we may have done so because we thought our spouses would _____: you fill in the blank.

We all have expectations going into marriage. We expect to be loved. We expect to be honored. We expect to be cherished. And there is nothing wrong with having these expectations. In fact, God has expectations for who we are to be in marriage. But marriages move from extraordinary to ordinary in the kinds of expectations we have of our spouses. Unrealistic or unfair expectations will always become unmet expectations.

When I expect my wife to have sex with me to cure my insecurity, that expectation will go unmet no matter how often we have sex. When my wife expects me to be home at five o'clock every night to ease her loneliness and depression, that expectation will go unmet no matter what time I come home. When we start expecting our spouses' words, behavior, or choices to fill parts of our hearts that only God can fill, we set ourselves up for ordinary marriages. That is exactly what Trisha and I were experiencing.

The root cause of unmet expectations is unrealistic and unfair expectations: the reverse messiah complex. We expect our spouses to fill voids in our lives or hearts that only God can fill. Unmet expectations reduce a journey expected to be amazing to ordinary. Unmet expectations breed hurt feelings, misunderstanding, and unresolved conflict.

How do you know if unmet expectations are leading you to an ordinary marriage? Below are some indications that one (or both) parties in your marriage may be suffering from a reverse messiah complex.

Keeping Score

One of the things I (Justin) love about being a dad is coaching my kids in sports. One year we enrolled Micah in Upward Basketball. Upward is a Christ-centered league that does a great job promoting teamwork and sportsmanship. The league is less about competition and more about fun. One of the ways that is expressed in younger age groups is by not keeping score on the scoreboard. So as the game goes on, the scoreboard never changes. It always reads 0–0. But the truth is that every parent and every coach silently keeps score and stats. So while everyone says they don't keep score, the score is still kept.

Unfortunately, the same thing is true in many marriages. We can be great scorekeepers. Our marriage scoreboards may say 0–0, but in our hearts, we *know* the score. We know exactly how much our spouses have to make up to us. We know exactly how far ahead we are. We take mental notes. We keep track. We can be great trash talkers too, because when we are ahead in the game, we have no problem letting our spouses know the score.

Keeping score is an indication that there are unmet expectations in your marriage. In basketball, without a hoop and net,

there's no goal, nothing to determine whether a scor
not. Similarly, in our marriages, without expectatio
be no way to tell whether our spouses have fallen sh
we make the effort to keep score, when marriage becomes a cu...
petition, you can be almost certain that the expectations are unfair
or unrealistic, and thus unmet.

Resignation & Defeat

Keeping score leads to a culture of resentment in a marriage. When
unfair and unmet expectations are part of your marriage, you probably won't fight about anything new. Why? Because when a husband
or wife has godlike expectations of the other person, there can never
be a resolution to that problem: no one can fill a God-sized hole but
God himself. The problem will keep coming back.

We don't often talk about the consequences of keeping score
and resentment, but they are very real. Most likely if you have a
scorekeeper in your marriage and if you are arguing about the same
things over and over again, then at least one of you fights the feeling
that no matter what you do, it is never enough. You feel defeated
more than you feel encouraged.

And this feeling of defeat becomes a self-fulfilling prophecy. You
begin to resign yourself to never being good enough. And if that's the
case, why even try? Resentment becomes resignation and defeat when
statements like these define your thoughts toward your marriage:

- No matter what I do, it is never good enough.
- No matter how much money I make, she's never satisfied.
- No matter how nice our house is, it's not big enough.
- No matter how often we have sex, it's never often enough.
- No matter what I wear, it's not good enough.
- No matter what chores I do, I never do them well enough.
- No matter what I make for dinner, it's not good enough.
- No matter how much I give, I don't give enough.
- No matter how much I listen, I never listen enough.

Resignation and defeat are indicators that there may be messiah-sized expectations in your marriage.

Absence of Conflict

When we have resigned ourselves to the probability that nothing we do will ever be good enough for our spouses, we start measuring the success of our marriage not by the presence of intimacy, but by the absence of conflict.

In our marriage, if Trisha and I (Justin) were able to get through a weekend without arguing . . . success! If I could go to a basketball game with some friends and not be made to feel guilty . . . success! If we spent an evening together at home and didn't argue about finances, chores, homework, overworking, or extended family issues, then our marriage, in my mind, was healthy. In other words, the success of our marriage was arranged around what we could avoid, rather than loving each other more deeply, knowing each other better, sharing our dreams more, understanding our passions, and growing our intimacy with one another. We looked for the absence of conflict rather than pursing the presence of intimacy. The truth is that we settled for so much less than God longed for us to experience as husband and wife.

I think that when most of us get married, we have a vision of growing in intimacy with our spouses. We believe that the longer we are married, the closer we will get to each other. But our extraordinary vision is too often replaced by ordinary reality. The goal we once had for intimacy quickly gets replaced with the goal of pain avoidance. We don't want to experience pain. We need a break, and we hope that avoiding conflict will bring some relief.

When pain avoidance becomes the goal, we start walking on eggshells and doing all we can to avoid an argument, to dodge conflict, to elude a disagreement. Avoiding pain will never lead to oneness. Dodging conflict will never allow us to be fully known. Our unreasonable and unfair expectations of our spouses in this way lead us down a path away from intimacy.

THE WAY OF THE DIP

When Moses rescued the people of Israel, they had e
They believed that life with God would be easier than l
Collectively, they had a belief that if life was not problem-free,
then God couldn't possibly be with them. Despite the burning
bush, despite the plagues, despite God's heart breaking over the
cries and prayers of his chosen people, the Israelites were ready to
reject God's rescue:

> As Pharaoh approached, the people of Israel looked up
> and panicked when they saw the Egyptians overtaking
> them. They cried out to the LORD, and they said to
> Moses, "Why did you bring us out here to die in the
> wilderness? Weren't there enough graves for us in Egypt?
> What have you done to us? Why did you make us leave
> Egypt? Didn't we tell you this would happen while we
> were still in Egypt? We said, 'Leave us alone! Let us be
> slaves to the Egyptians. It's better to be a slave in Egypt
> than a corpse in the wilderness!'"
> EXODUS 14:10-12

In other words, the Israelites said, "We would prefer the absence
of conflict, working as slaves in Egypt, to intimacy with God in
the uncertainty of the wilderness." And it's no different with us.
We will always be tempted to settle for ordinary in Egypt rather
than walking with God through the wilderness to extraordinary.

But God's greatest purpose for the people of Israel wasn't where
they were going; it was who they were becoming. God was willing
to allow a nineteen-day journey from Egypt to Canaan to take
forty years, not because he is bad with directions but because he
is great with character development. God's wilderness detour was
intended to refine the Israelites and to teach them more about
who God is. The Israelites needed to learn to love and trust God

through his provision in the wilderness so that they wouldn't forget him in the Promised Land. In fact, God tells them that when they are fully provided for is the "time to be careful":

> Beware that in your plenty you do not forget the LORD your God and disobey his commands, regulations, and decrees that I am giving you today. For when you have become full and prosperous and have built fine homes to live in, and when your flocks and herds have become very large and your silver and gold have multiplied along with everything else, be careful! Do not become proud at that time and forget the LORD your God, who rescued you from slavery in the land of Egypt. Do not forget that he led you through the great and terrifying wilderness with its poisonous snakes and scorpions, where it was so hot and dry. He gave you water from the rock! He fed you with manna in the wilderness, a food unknown to your ancestors. He did this to humble you and test you for your own good. He did all this so you would never say to yourself, "I have achieved this wealth with my own strength and energy." Remember the LORD your God. He is the one who gives you power to be successful, in order to fulfill the covenant he confirmed to your ancestors with an oath.
> DEUTERONOMY 8:11-18

Seth Godin, in his book *The Dip: A Little Book That Teaches You When to Quit (and When to Stick)*, writes about this tendency:

> Almost everything in life worth doing is controlled by the Dip. . . .
> At the beginning, when you first start something, it's fun. You could be taking up golf or acupuncture or piloting a plane or doing chemistry—doesn't matter; it's

interesting, and you get plenty of good feedback from the people around you.

Over the next few days and weeks, the rapid learning you experience keeps you going. Whatever your new thing is, it's easy to stay engaged in it.

And then the Dip happens.

The Dip is the long slog between starting and mastery. A long slog that's actually a shortcut, because it gets you where you want to go faster than any other path. . . .

Successful people don't just ride out the Dip. They don't just buckle down and survive it. No, they lean into the Dip. They push harder, changing the rules as they go.

Our tendency is to assume that if we stay together, our marriages will get easier. But the reality is that longer doesn't equal easier. More years married doesn't necessarily equal more happiness.

Telling the truth is difficult. Forgiveness is painful. The people we love the most drive us the most crazy. When our marriages don't play out as we think they should, we are left discouraged and questioning our decision. That is the Dip. That is the place where we feel defeated. That is the place we feel helpless. That is the place where we have manipulated all we can and our spouses aren't changing. That is the place where our milestones and achievements don't fix our problems. That is the place where we stand at a crossroads and are given the choice: go back to life in Egypt, which is really no life at all, or trust God through the wilderness. That is the place where we have to choose to stick it out or to quit.

Walking through the Dip seems counter to our vision of what we thought marriage would be. We said, "for better or worse," but we probably thought it would just be "better." The Dip challenges our preconceived notions of marriage and causes us to ask, "Is it worth it?" The Dip is a path paved with honesty and hurt and vulnerability and risk and mistakes and insecurity and raw conversations.

The Dip is not the path of least resistance. But it is in the dips that God shapes us, forms us, and refines us. The Dip feels like something we should get out of as quickly as possible, something we should avoid. What we think is that by not walking with God and our spouses through the Dip, we are saving ourselves from pain and hurt. But what we forfeit by not embracing the Dip is God's molding and forming our hearts.

It is the moments when we embrace the downward turns in marriage that God gives us the marriages we had dreamed of; not because he has changed our spouses, but because we are allowing him to change us. In those challenging moments of embracing the Dip, we learn to lean on God rather than trying to be god. We allow God to remake our expectations and to transform our vision of who God is, who we are, and who our spouses are. Ordinary marriages go to great lengths to avoid marriage valleys, yet it is often in the valleys that God meets us and sets us up for extraordinary.

QUESTIONS

1. Messiah complex or reverse messiah complex: Which best describes your role in your marriage?

2. Are you a scorekeeper? If so, what specific areas in your relationship do you tend to keep score of?

3. What conditions and expectations are there in your marriage? Are they reasonable?

4. What was a time your marriage faced "the Dip"? Did you embrace it or avoid it? How might your marriage be different if you had taken another path?

5.

NO ORDINARY CONTRACT

AS I (JUSTIN) WRITE this chapter, only a few weeks remain before the second biggest day in Indianapolis Colts history. The biggest day in Colts history was the day they drafted Peyton Manning. That was the day the Colts became contenders. It was the day people started respecting our team. It was a beautiful day. The second biggest day in Colts history will be the day they decide whether they will waive Peyton Manning because they don't believe he can play at the level he once did, or whether they are going to pay him the twenty-eight-million-dollar bonus he is due to keep him on the team.

As a fan not just of the Colts but of Peyton Manning, I think to myself, *How did it come to this?* I remember people lining the streets in subzero temperatures just a few years ago to celebrate the Super Bowl victory that Peyton brought to our city. I remember watching as the children's hospital in Indianapolis was renamed the

Peyton Manning Children's Hospital because of the investment he made both financially and with his time. Every week there seemed to be a story on the news about all that Peyton's PeyBack Foundation was doing for underprivileged kids in the city. Not only can I not imagine Peyton playing for another team, I can't imagine him being part of another city.

As a fan, I don't think of Peyton Manning as being under contract with the Colts. It's like he's a part of us not because he is paid to be, but because he chooses to be. It's like he's in covenant with the Colts, the city of Indianapolis, and the fans. Yeah, he signed a piece of paper, but his allegiance seems to transcend contract. It's like both he and the Colts promised to be together.

But that isn't the reality. Peyton Manning and the Colts aren't in a covenant relationship; they are in a contractual agreement. Contracts expire. Contracts can be renegotiated. (And, in fact, the Colts *did* release Manning, and he signed a new contract with the Denver Broncos.) But a covenant, by its very nature, should last forever.

When we get married, our vision is covenant. We make promises. We recite vows. We commit to being there for our spouses. We swear to love unconditionally, "in sickness and in health." We are not signing a contract, with a series of clauses, exemptions, and meticulous details that can be renegotiated and appealed to. We are entering a covenant, born from the love in our hearts, which is unconcerned with particulars. This covenant feels right. This covenant feels holy. This covenant feels ordained. We're not as concerned with what we get as with what we have to give.

Extraordinary flows from covenant, ordinary from contract. Ordinary isn't something we choose; it's something that happens by not choosing extraordinary.

Trisha and I had drifted to an ordinary place in our marriage because we didn't choose covenant. We drifted to and existed in a contract mentality. When we chose to allow our marriage to be a contractual agreement, ordinary was only a matter of time.

TRISHA:

After three years of marriage, we achieved a dream that took our parents fifteen years of marriage to accomplish: we bought our first house. Kokomo, Indiana, was not only known for being a hub for the auto industry, it was also an inexpensive place to live. We bought our eleven-hundred-square-foot home for a whopping sixty thousand dollars. The carpet and wall color were as old as the house itself, but they were ours, and we loved them. With baby boy number two on the way, orange walls and green carpeting never looked so good.

The fall and winter of 1998 are all a blur. Pregnant and wrangling an active toddler, I took most of that time to unpack and get settled. With our son Elijah due to arrive at the end of March, there was a sense of anticipation in our house. This time we were ready. This time we had the money, time, and space to do things right. This time Justin and I felt a sense of pride because we were "old enough" to be parents.

That spring brought about more than just the birth of our precious Elijah. It brought the first sightings of the Promised Land. Over the next few years, our search for community and relevant ministry would come to fruition. It was here in Kokomo that I could finally sigh and say, "We've made it." Our time in the desert, of Justin's searching for the perfect ministry, was coming to an end.

As the flowers in our front yard bloomed, so did my heart. After investing in friends and students in our prior ministries, I struggled to fully embrace other people, fearing I would only have to leave them after a year or two had passed. I had promised myself I wouldn't seek out friends as I had in the past. But my new church would hear nothing of it. I was engulfed by staff and students and even found my kindred spirit. This kindred spirit was everything I wasn't, but as the saying goes, opposites attract. What we did have in common was that we were both young marrieds in love with our husbands and devoted to our children.

With my kindred spirit's family, nobody was a stranger, and she made no exception to this rule when it came to my family. Only three months after our move, her family invited us to Christmas dinner. I was still pregnant and unable to stomach the smell of marinara, so they turned their usual Christmas pasta dinner into one that was free of red sauce. What was likely a small sacrifice for them was a huge push to move me toward fully embracing community. By spring, this kindred spirit had become my best friend, and I loved every minute of our friendship!

One of the ways our friendship grew and solidified was over cupcakes. When Justin and I started at the church, a lot of the women there were pregnant and nearing the date for their baby showers. It was so fun celebrating the births of all these babies, and I was becoming a baby shower expert. But there is one shower I will never forget.

My best friend, who is an amazing cook—unlike me (I had an older sibling to take care of the cooking duties when I was younger)—had asked me to bake some cupcakes for an upcoming shower. She would bake some as well, and we would combine them to make a cake tower. As I entered my best friend's house, she could tell I was disappointed in my cupcakes' less-than-appealing appearance. Hers were fluffy and pretty; mine were wimpy and disfigured. After my initial moment of disappointment passed, we laughed at how bad they looked. But she graciously took my contribution and hid them in the inner part of the tower, somehow making the whole thing look *Better Homes and Gardens* worthy.

This was one of my favorite things about her. When I was my worst critic, she was always there to provide an encouraging perspective. I was finally getting to experience the potential of not just being a friend, but having a friend.

I was that kid who loved to do things as a team—and I still am. Personal achievement didn't give as much of a "high" as accomplishing something as a team. In middle school, our band didn't have a flag team, so I started one. In high school, we lost our dance coach due to a failed referendum, but I didn't let that stop me. I gathered our team, found a teacher to drive us, and we went to camp anyway. Not only did we go to camp, we won a spot to go to nationals, where we eventually placed. Being married to a pastor was no different. Justin and I partnered together to change the world through the local church, and I *loved* being in ministry together.

When I was in elementary school, my cousin Melissa and I sang together at church on Mother's Day. We stood on top of two small wooden chairs in order to see over the pulpit and sang a song that spelled out *mother*. To this day Melissa laughs hysterically when we talk about it because after the song I yelled into the mic, "Can you tell what word we just spelled?" Fortunately for me, this little burst of comedy wasn't held against me, and I continued to sing from behind that pulpit until I left for college.

I never wanted to be a famous singer, songwriter, or musician, but what I loved about singing was that I got to sing with my brother. He has one of the purest voices I've ever heard. I *loved* being his background singer, and I was content with being just that. Now that I was married and in ministry, I still found myself singing behind a pulpit, even if the pulpits changed from year to year. When we moved to Kokomo, not only did I find my best friend, I also found my voice, not as a background singer, but as a worship leader. Our senior pastor, Mark, was constantly pushing me to lead songs. I didn't have much of an idea what he meant, but I knew that I loved to help our congregation connect to the song I was about to sing. There is something precious when you get to see a song connect a person's heart to God's. Getting to sing a song after I spoke was the icing on the cake. God used Mark and my church family to unlock another passion in me that I didn't even know existed. The Promised Land just kept getting better.

But I could see a sandstorm in the far distance, and what I had come to learn is that the only place you find sand is the desert. As much as I felt built up by friends and my church family, I felt like Justin never matched their intensity in loving me. My

ke they wanted to be around me. Justin seemed
to help him build his ministry.

to our time in Kokomo, the issues that had
Justin in previous ministries were making a comeback. He
didn't feel respected. He had a hard time feeling satisfied. As Justin
struggled, the people I had learned to trust became the standard to
which Justin constantly compared me. Justin made comments that
let me know that in his eyes I wasn't good enough, and I filed them
away in my heart. It seemed that he utilized my gifts only to the
extent that they benefited his ministry—until a staff member or
volunteer came along who could do it better. Even more hurtful,
my best friend seemed to always be the first in Justin's comparison
lineup. My best friend was everything I wasn't, but that's what I
loved about her, and I knew she felt the same about me. But Justin
was quick to criticize the areas where I seemed to fail at home
because he saw her do it better. Out of self-protection and in keeping with the spirit of "team," I said nothing. My self-preservation
solidified to the extent that it felt like Justin and I were no longer
in a covenant relationship but rather a contractual agreement. Our
relationship had become daily talks of negotiations about what we
needed from each other rather than offering how we could serve
one another. I was settling for ordinary.

JUSTIN:

When I think about my life, I can't help but regret all the time I
wasted in discontentment. This has impacted many areas of my
life, but one of the hardest hit was my marriage. Without even
realizing it, I started to compare Trisha to her best friend. Why
couldn't Trisha cook like her? Why couldn't Trisha work part-time
like her? Why wasn't she wired like her? This comparison started
out lightheartedly and then made its way into arguments—which
would then cause more arguments.

My discontentment went way beyond our marriage, though. It

started in my relationship with God and bled into all aspects of my life. Comparing Trisha to her best friend was not an isolated occurrence. No matter what area of my life I examined, I was discontented.

By God's grace, we were able to purchase our first house in Kokomo. It was an amazing house, and we had everything we needed. Three bedrooms, a fenced-in backyard, a great neighborhood—yet it wasn't enough, at least not for me. Two years into our time there, I wanted a bigger house. I wanted a basement. I wanted a man cave. I wanted multiple bathrooms. I wanted nicer carpet. I wanted a bigger yard.

I felt the same discontent about our student ministry. When we arrived in Kokomo, the church was growing and exciting. The student ministry, however, had a healthy core group of students, but it wasn't growing. Our first Sunday, we had twenty-three students show up—sitting in our five-hundred-seat auditorium. At the very end of the message, I asked them to close their eyes. I asked them to imagine the auditorium we were sitting in filled with students. I asked them to imagine a place where their friends could come on Sunday nights and experience God in a real and fresh way. I told them that God had a plan for their school. God had a plan for their friends. God had a plan for every single student in their lunchroom. God had a plan for every single student in their biology class. God's plan for their friends hinged on the students' willingness to partner with God to share his love with them.

What happened over the next year was a total God thing. Those twenty-three students believed what I said. They invited their friends. They owned our vision. They served and shared and invested. Our group of twenty-three became a group of fifty. Our group of fifty became a group of one hundred. Within two years of our moving to Kokomo, we had over two hundred students in the ministry and seventy-five adult volunteers. Students who were far from God came to our church and found grace in a relationship with Christ. We launched multiple small groups and had amazing adult leaders who were investing every single week in the lives of students.

Trisha was an integral part of this movement. Early on, she was our worship leader. As the ministry grew, she trained our students to lead worship. Eventually, we had a student band and several student worship teams. As that need was met, Trisha led a group of freshman girls. She was an amazing small-group leader and had a vision of being with these girls all the way through graduation. We hadn't stayed at our previous ministries long enough to see many students graduate, and that was a prospect she was passionate about.

As Trisha became more invested in our ministry, I became more discontented. God was blessing our ministry in amazing ways, but it wasn't enough for me. No matter how many students showed up, it wasn't enough. No matter how great a service was on a particular Sunday night, we had to top it the next week. No matter how many compliments I was given by the staff or by our volunteers, they weren't respecting me enough. Maybe this wasn't the right ministry for me? Maybe I'd be happier somewhere else? Maybe God could use my gifts in greater ways at a bigger church?

Discontentment with our house, our church, and our marriage had made its home in my heart.

JUSTIN & TRISHA:

THE GOD OF THE COVENANT

A covenant is different from a contract. While a contract has an element of commitment and promise attached to it, most contracts are conditional, temporary, and breakable. The heart of a covenant is different. It is based on the promise of those who enter it and their desire for it to be without conditions. In the Bible, God moves beyond the letter of the law of contract and initiates the covenant. He promises, unconditionally, to be faithful and to be the God of his people.

God's vision for his relationship with us is a covenant. He is to be our God, and we are to be his people. In Genesis, God makes two covenants—two promises. He promises Noah that he will never again destroy the earth by flood. Later in the book of Genesis, God makes what many consider the most important covenant in the Old Testament: he promises Abraham that he will make him a great nation and will bless all nations through Abraham. With that covenant, the nation of Israel is born. He later makes a covenant with Moses to lead the Israelites to the Promised Land. And later still, God promises King David that his descendants will be the line from which the Messiah will come.

The birth, life, death, and resurrection of Jesus ushered in what we call the *new covenant*. In this new covenant—this new promise—God promises to make us right with him through his grace and mercy, purchased by Jesus' sacrifice on the cross. It is now possible to be forgiven for our sins through the person of Jesus Christ. Jesus' sacrifice on the cross is the fruition of this new covenant.

Unlike a contract, the covenant Jesus offers doesn't expire. This promise doesn't have to be renegotiated. Once we enter into a covenant relationship with Jesus, this promise is forever.

If you look throughout the Bible, you'll see that even though God's desire was to live in a covenant relationship with his people, his people were not good promise keepers. They were always breaking their promises. They promised to have no other gods before him (Exodus 20:3-4; 24:3), but then they made idols (Exodus 32:1-6). They promised to follow God's law and meditate on it day and night (Deuteronomy 6:4-9), and then they did evil in the eyes of the Lord (Judges 2:11). They promised to trust God and put their faith in him, and then they questioned his presence and his plan.

While God viewed his relationship with his people as a covenant, they viewed their relationship with God as a contract. It is one of the reasons why Jesus told the parable of the Prodigal (or Lost) Son, which is really about *two* lost sons. We obviously think of this story as an example of God's amazing grace to those who are far from him as shown in the Prodigal Son himself. But Jesus inserts the character of the older brother to illustrate our tendency to think contractually about God.

[The older brother] replied, "All these years I've slaved for you and never once refused to do a single thing you told me to. And in all that time you never gave me even one young goat for a feast with my friends. Yet when this son of yours comes back after squandering your money on prostitutes, you celebrate by killing the fattened calf!"

LUKE 15:29-30

The older brother's relationship with his father has obviously cooled to the point of contract at this point. The older brother is angry that his father lavishes such love on someone who has shirked his responsibilities, while the responsible one is living as a second-class citizen in his own home. But the father in the story explains the reality of the situation: "Look, dear son, you have always stayed by me, and everything I have is yours" (Luke 15:31). The older brother may not have gone to a "distant land" (Luke 15:13) like his younger brother, but he was there in his heart: he had forsaken the gifts his father had already given him. The father and the older son's contractual relationship was one sided. The offer of covenant was always full and complete on the father's part; the older son refused to accept it, turning the covenant into a contract.

While God desires covenant, humans have an uncanny ability to turn a covenant relationship into a contractual agreement. We're really good at it in our relationships with God, and if we are honest, we do the same thing in our marriages.

DISCONTENTMENT & CONTRACTUAL MARRIAGES

One of the signs of a marriage moving from a covenant to a contract is discontentment. In the last chapter, we talked about unrealistic and unfair expectations, and discontentment is in many ways related to unmet expectations. Allowing unmet expectations to continue in our marriage creates a snowball effect into discontentment.

The problem with discontentment is that it convinces us that if we were just a little bit more of this, or had a little bit more of that, or accomplished a little bit more of something else, then we would be content. But discontentment is hard to satisfy, and it will turn any great marriage into an ordinary marriage.

Discontentment lives in the fine print of a contractual marriage. When we have contractual marriages, we are never really satisfied. Our spouses are never quite good enough. They don't fold the laundry up to our standards. They don't keep the house as clean as we would like it. They don't manage the finances up to our expectations. They could always be a little more in shape, a little more put together, a little more like someone else. Discontentment tries to convince us that we would be happier with something new, something else.

When we first get married, we are so impressed with all that our spouses are. We love their sense of humor; we admire their ability to take risks. We are blown away by their organizational skills. We are attracted to their laid-back attitude and disposition. It seems that everything they are is everything we aren't. They are punctual; we are fashionably late. They are emotional; we are logical. They are impulsive; we are calculated. There is a deep sense within us that all of their strengths are all of our weaknesses, and that we complement one another feels really good. They will complete us. Or so we believe.

Over time, the strengths we saw in our spouses that complemented our weaknesses become weaknesses that complicate our strengths. We resent that they are laid back. We get mad that they always have to be on time. We hate the way they lay out their clothes before they go to bed, or how outgoing they are, or all the risks they are willing to take. What was once attractive now creates a sense of discontentment in our hearts. They aren't good enough. They aren't sensitive enough. They aren't pretty enough. They aren't interesting enough. Discontentment always pushes us to compare what we have to what someone else has. Even more dangerous, discontentment will always push us to compare who our spouses are to who someone else is.

But comparison is never about the person we are comparing to someone else. It is always about our own hearts. Where discontentment lives, brokenness thrives.

THE SUBTLE TRAP OF ENTITLEMENT

Discontentment leads to entitlement. Entitlement sets the tone that when our spouses fail to meet our expectations, we're owed even more. Entitlement becomes the catalyst for remaining in ordinary. Entitlement permits us to take control of the situation from our spouses and from God. Entitlement cloaks the belief that we are the better spouse and make an even better god.

As Moses led the Israelites out of Egypt, God provided for their every need. In fact, he provided for their needs in supernatural ways. When the Israelites were thirsty, he made the bitter water taste good. When they were hungry, he rained down food from heaven and even rained down a double portion on the sixth day so they could honor the Sabbath. Food *rained down* from heaven—my (Trisha's) dream come true. They didn't have to plant it, harvest it, or process it; they just had to pick it up. Yet it was never enough. No matter what the Lord provided, the Israelites felt entitled to more. As a result of their constant feelings of entitlement, when the Lord didn't provide for them in exactly the way they wanted, the Israelites sought their own means of fulfillment, breaking God's laws and severing their relationship with God in the process.

In Exodus 33, we find Moses in an intense conversation with God. Because of his frustrations with the Israelites, God says he will send an angel with them into battle, but he will not go with them himself. He has tried to live in covenant with them, yet they continually opt for a contractual agreement. He's not going back on his promise, but how he gives his promise is about to change.

The LORD said to Moses, "Leave this place, you and the people you brought up out of Egypt, and go up to the land I promised on oath to Abraham, Isaac and Jacob, saying, 'I will give it to your descendants.' I will send an angel before you and drive out the Canaanites, Amorites, Hittites, Perizzites, Hivites and Jebusites. Go up to the land flowing with milk and honey. But I will not go with you, because you are a stiff-necked people and I might destroy you on the way." . . .

Then Moses said to him, "If your Presence does not go with us, do not send us up from here. How will anyone know that you are pleased with me and with your people unless you go with us? What else will distinguish me and your people from all the other people on the face of the earth?"

EXODUS 33:1-3, 15-16, NIV

The Israelites might have missed the point, but Moses saw the bigger picture. He knew that without God, it didn't matter what the Israelites did or didn't have. Nothing would be better than the presence of God.

But much like the Israelites, we can easily stop focusing on the *presence* of God and focus instead on the *presents* of God. We exchange the joys of the covenant for the drudgeries of the contract. And when we live in contractual relationships with God, it should come as no surprise that we live in contractual relationships with our spouses. We turn our disappointments into ransom notes for our hearts: our spouses must either give us what we want to get love from us or get nothing at all. When we take our eyes off God, we lose sight of the gift that our spouses *are* and focus on the gifts they aren't giving us.

ENTITLEMENT'S THREE FAVORITE WORDS

Entitlement's three favorite words are *You. Owe. Me.*

Trisha and I made the decision from the time we knew she was pregnant with Micah that she would stay home with our kids. She wanted to be a stay-at-home mom. She grew up in a family where both parents worked outside the home, and I grew up with a stay-at-home mom. So for each of us, in our own way, it was important for us to have Trisha stay home.

Maybe all husbands struggle with entitlement when their wives stay home. If they do, not many talk about it. I really struggled. I had this feeling that because I went to work and Trisha "got" to stay home, she owed me. I expected her to help in my ministry—to be a wife and a mom full time but then to fill holes as a small group leader or as a worship leader in our ministry. At first, my intentions were pure and good. But over time, my expectation came from a place of entitlement.

I had this deep-seated attitude that Trisha had to pay me back for me "allowing" her to stay home. I was doing her a favor. She should be grateful for what I was doing for her.

Entitlement allows gratitude and the mutual submission of a covenant to evaporate from a marriage, and it always knows what your spouse has to do to make it up to you.

- You want to go out with your friends? You owe me.
- You want to go shopping with your sister? You owe me.
- You want me to watch the kids so you can have a night out? You owe me.
- You expect to have dinner on the table when you get home? You owe me.
- You want me to work longer hours so you can be a stay-at-home mom? You owe me.
- You want me to have sex with you when I don't feel like it? You owe me.
- You like having clean clothes in your closet each week? You owe me.
- You want me to come home early so you can go to the movies? You owe me.

Most of us get married with a high sense of grati/ time goes on, everything we used to be grateful for . feel entitled to. You can't simultaneously be grateful for something and feel entitled to it.

Entitlement quietly turns extraordinary marriages into ordinary ones. Entitlement turns teammates into opponents. Entitlement allows us to overlook what we can give to a relationship and see only what we are owed by the other in the relationship. Entitlement enables us to believe that what we deserve is greater than what we should be thankful for. When entitlement sets into our hearts, ordinary is soon to follow.

Contractual agreements have stipulations and contingencies. If those contingencies aren't met, then you are free to break the contract. You have an out. It's telling that conditions and stipulations never make their way into our weddings, but they often take center stage in our marriages.

OUR PATH TO CHANGE

A lot of married couples who struggle with comparison and entitlement have good intentions. Wait a second: How can we have good intentions when we compare our spouses to someone else? How can spouses who have entitlement issues have good intentions? It is easy for those of us who are married to believe that comparisons and entitlement will bring the changes to our marriages that we desire. We think that our marriages will be different if our spouses' behavior changes. We think our marriages will be different if our spouses finally give us what they owe us. Our underlying desire is a better marriage (which is good), but our problem is self-centered hearts (which is not).

Changes in our marriages don't come by changing our spouses' behavior; they come by allowing God to change our hearts. In failing to pursue that transformation, discontentment, comparison, and entitlement are the fool's gold we settle for. The problem is that instead of bringing us to extraordinary, they work together to leave us in ordinary.

Ordinary, because it is in many ways contractual, can see divorce as an option. Ordinary has no problem with contingencies and contingency plans. Ordinary allows us to picture ourselves with someone else. Ordinary leaves us never satisfied. Ordinary brings us to a place where we can't love or receive love unconditionally. Ordinary makes us believe it's okay to compare our spouses to someone else. Ordinary narrows our vision to see only the things that bother us about our spouses and forget the reasons why we love them. Ordinary leaves our marriages existing but not fulfilling.

GOD'S PATH TO CHANGE

God's desire from the beginning has been to live in covenant with us. His desire for your marriage is for you and your spouse to live in covenant with each other. All the contracts in the world—with their rules, contingencies, and stipulations—won't give you an extraordinary marriage.

Through Jesus, we have the promise of a new covenant. Maybe you need to have a new covenant in your marriage, as well. Maybe you need to stop trying to create an extraordinary marriage from an ordinary contractual system. What would be different if you started living and loving from a covenant?

While it might seem like a cliché, the best picture of a covenant marriage is found in 1 Corinthians 13:4-7:

Love is patient and kind. Love is not jealous or boastful or proud or rude. It does not demand its own way. It is not irritable, and it keeps no record of being wronged. It does not rejoice about injustice but rejoices whenever the truth wins out. Love never gives up, never loses faith, is always hopeful, and endures through every circumstance.

This description isn't something that just sounds good when read at weddings. It is God's plan and God's vision for a covenant marriage. Marriages built on contractual agreements will always fall short of these covenant ideals.

But you might be wondering, what if your husband doesn't do his part? It is a risk. What if your wife still takes advantage of you? It is a possibility. What if your spouse doesn't change his or her behavior, even though you removed your conditions and stipulations? It could happen. But look at it this way: you can't keep doing what you've always done and expect a different result.

That was the biggest mistake Trisha and I (Justin) made. We thought we could do more of what we'd always done and have a different marriage. We only improved at being dysfunctional. We only got better at ordinary. Trisha and I found ourselves surrounded with everything that should have given us an extraordinary marriage: a great home, good friends, a Christ-centered church, a growing ministry, and a marriage that appeared healthy. Despite all of that, I needed more. Despite all of that, Trisha couldn't convince me it was enough.

QUESTIONS

1. Which best describes your marriage relationship: covenant or contract? In what way(s) does this description fit?

2. What role does discontentment have in your life and marriage?

3. In what areas do you feel entitled in your marriage? How does this sense of entitlement reveal itself?

4. What steps can you take to make your marriage more covenant than contract?

6.

NO ORDINARY CROSSROADS

THE STORY OF SAMSON (Judges 13–16) is a story of unrealized potential. Yet Samson was always presented in a heroic way in Sunday school. He was a champion sent by God to rescue God's people. He was like He-Man before there was He-Man. Yes, he got his eyes plucked out and lost his strength, yet God still allowed him to push the pillars of the pagan temple over and crush the Philistines. He sacrificed himself to save his people.

When that story was told in Sunday school, it made little kids everywhere want to lift weights, grow their hair long, and knock down buildings with their bare hands. But when you read his entire story, you realize it is the story of what might have been. It is the story of a man who, because of his own poor choices, sacrificed something God never intended him to sacrifice.

An angel appeared to Samson's parents before he was born and predicted his birth. The angel commanded Samson's mom to not drink any alcohol or eat any forbidden food. In addition, the angel instructed Samson's mom to raise Samson as a strict Nazirite (see Numbers 6). Nazirites were to make three commitments:

- they could not cut their hair;
- they could not drink alcohol; and
- they could not touch a dead body.

Submitting to God in this Nazirite vow would be the source of the strength Samson needed to accomplish the mission God had given him. His commitment to the vow would allow him to realize his potential and save Israel from its enemies.

But while Samson had tremendous physical strength, he had weakness of character. When giftedness outweighs character, implosion isn't a matter of *if* but of *when*. Samson was impulsive. He saw something, he desired it, and he did whatever he had to do to get it.

Samson saw a Philistine woman. He went home and told his mother and father that he wanted to marry her. His father protested and encouraged him to marry an Israelite, but Samson insisted that he marry the Philistine. "Get her for me," he said. "She is the one I want."

See. Want. Get.

A lion attacked Samson, and the Bible says that he ripped the lion apart with his bare hands. By any standard, that is impressive. Later he went back and saw that bees had made a hive in the carcass of the lion. Samson scooped some honey out of the lion's carcass and ate it, even giving some to his parents. But Samson wasn't supposed to touch anything dead, and he made a decision in this moment that he would repeat throughout his life: he chose not to tell his parents that he had broken his vow and touched a dead animal.

See. Want. Get.

Some would call Samson driven, but his drive was often irresponsible. While being driven can be a good thing, it can also be destructive. Sometimes it isn't the big decisions we make that rob us of our potential, it is the small compromises along the way, the impulsive things we do that don't seem like that big of a deal but that bring consequences far bigger than we could imagine. Samson is a picture of hidden impulses and uncontrolled desires that rob people of their potential.

Samson's pattern of see, want, get was unfortunately reproduced in our marriage, and it had similar potential-destroying effects.

JUSTIN:

Potential is a loaded word. In my mind potential has always been tied to significance. The greater your potential, the greater your ability to be significant. All through college, my professors told me how much potential I had. Usually, though, I was told this in a conversation that took place after I had missed too many classes, gotten a low grade on an exam, or turned a paper in late. It was more about what could have been than the potential I had realized.

When I got into ministry, the word *potential* came up often. After I would speak on a Sunday morning, an older person in the congregation would tell me how much potential I had. What I heard when they tossed out *potential* was, "Someday you'll be a good speaker." Potential reared its ambivalent head in performance reviews as well. I felt cursed at times because the gifts and abilities I had were enough to impress those I worked for, but the weaknesses and blind spots were enough to frustrate them. "Your potential is off the charts. If only you were more organized." "You have so much potential. If only you were more responsible." Potential felt like a backhanded compliment. In my mind, when someone wanted to tell me how far short I had fallen from their expectations, they used the word *potential*. I had the potential to be a great leader, pastor, and speaker. Achieving my potential became the pursuit of my heart. I was more concerned with what I could accomplish than with who I was becoming.

Potential was a pretty big word for our marriage as well. Our marriage had tons of potential. Two gifted people in love with Christ, his church, and each other. Now six years into our marriage, I felt like my role as a husband was more a picture of potential lost than potential realized. "You'd be a really good husband if you were home on time." "You'd be an amazing husband if you would pick up your underwear." "You'd be a perfect husband if you could calm my fears and take away my insecurities." Not realizing potential professionally or in my marriage didn't just make me feel like a failure, it allowed me to see how close I came to being successful, yet still falling short.

It was especially difficult when I compared my potential to Trisha's. While Trisha was feeling valued in our ministry and church in Kokomo, I was feeling taken advantage of. As people in the church grew in their respect for Trisha, I felt disrespected by staff members and volunteers. While Trisha was realizing her dream of being known and knowing others, I feared being found out.

One night after youth group, one of the volunteers in our ministry asked Trisha if she could come over to our house. I arrived home to find her and Trisha sitting on the couch talking. I quickly realized that she wasn't there to talk to Trish; she was there to talk to me. Courageously and humbly, she talked to me about my role as a pastor and how much she looked up to me. But she had noticed several times in the past few months when she knew I had stretched the truth or had not been entirely honest.

She was right. It wasn't that I was lying about big things. I had exaggerated parts of a conversation. I'd left out details of a story. I'd added information that would make me look good or sound spiritual or impress people. All of it was small and subtle, but this volunteer had spent enough time with me to notice, and my credibility was questioned as a result.

She told me that she had talked to our senior pastor about it, and he had encouraged her to speak the truth in love to me in the presence of Trisha. In that moment, I felt caught. Trish had already questioned my ability to share all the details of a conversation. She knew I would frequently fabricate or embellish a story while I was speaking. We had talked about it, and I had blown her off. I thought she was overreacting. But now, not only did my wife know the truth about me, the senior pastor knew, and I was convinced that he would tell the entire staff. I didn't feel known—I felt found out.

I stood at a crossroads in the area of integrity. I could own my mistakes and admit my faults, or I could try to talk my way out of them.

The next day I had a meeting with our senior pastor, and I tried to justify the partial truths I had been telling. I wasn't sorry for what I had done; I was sorry I had been caught. This church didn't value me, I thought. They didn't know what a great gift they had in me. They only wanted to point out my weaknesses. It felt like everyone there was out to get me, and I wanted to leave. A new start was what I needed.

TRISHA:

It's true that pastors, professors, friends, and family saw great potential in Justin, but I was his number one fan. *Twilight* fans may choose Team Edward or Team Jacob, but I was Team Justin all the way. The potential in Justin and my passion for team living were like fuel to a fire, and I loved seeing Justin shine brightly.

When Justin said we were moving from Illinois to Ohio, I knew we would do great things. When we moved from Ohio back to Illinois, I knew we could do even greater things. But when we moved from Illinois to Indiana, I knew we would do the impossible, and in our first three years in Kokomo, we felt like we were doing just that.

Still, I knew that some of the problems Justin had faced before were making a comeback. But I thought that because our ministry—and our family—was thriving in Kokomo, there was no way Justin would want out.

When Justin mentioned, out of the blue, that he was talking to a church in Nashville about a youth pastor position, Team Justin was about to become a one-on-one contact sport. No longer was I for Team Justin. I was becoming his enemy.

I loved our home, our ministry, and our church family. I couldn't imagine leaving. Justin framed the conversation about the move saying that it was God's will, but how could God be calling him to something greater when what Justin was already doing seemed so great? I knew Justin still had untapped potential, but did we really have to move to Nashville to see him achieve it? It was difficult to discern what was God's will and what was simply hidden impulses and uncontrolled desires. Then again, who was I to get in the way of the bigger picture that God might have for us?

In keeping with team spirit and being obedient to what we thought was God's will, we moved again—but this time not as teammates. I had checked out of the game altogether.

JUSTIN:

The more my character came into question, the more I felt disrespected by our staff and by Trisha. They didn't truly appreciate what I was accomplishing. At the same time, my best friend and our student ministry worship pastor, Kerry, came to tell me he was resigning in order to move to Colorado to help start a church. Kerry was instrumental in the growth we were experiencing in Kokomo. Students were drawn to the culture of worship Kerry had created. He was going to be missed. I had no idea how to replace him.

One afternoon my senior pastor came into my office and handed me a phone number. He told me that a friend of his was on staff at a church in Nashville and that he might be a good contact to find Kerry's replacement. I had no other leads, so this seemed like a great idea.

I called the number Mark gave me. "Hello, this is Pete." The name on the paper was Eddie. Maybe I had the wrong extension?

"Hi, Pete," I said. "This is Justin Davis. I'm looking for Eddie."

"Eddie just resigned," Pete said, "and I've taken his place."

This was odd, but I was desperate. I shared my situation with him and that I was looking for a student worship leader for our ministry. I told him of the growth we had experienced over the past two years and that this could be a really good position for the right person.

Pete said, "I'm new here, and I honestly don't know of anyone who would be a good fit. I am looking for a youth pastor here, though, so if you know of anyone I could talk to, please let me know."

We talked a few more minutes, and he told me about the church and the position. I told him I would let him know if someone came to mind.

A few days later, Pete called me back. "Have you given the youth pastor position any more thought?"

"Not really," I said. "I don't know anyone who would be a good fit."

"What about you?" Pete asked. "Why don't you apply? You'd be perfect for this position."

I was a bit taken aback. I told him, "If you don't mind hiring a divorced youth pastor, then I might apply."

"You're divorced?" Pete asked.

"I will be if I try to move my wife again," I said, only half joking. "It's just not going to happen." We hung up that day, and I didn't give Pete's suggestion much thought.

A few days later, Pete called me again. We talked about the church he had planted in Kentucky and his philosophy of ministry. We had a lot in common, and we got along really well. A few days later, we talked again. I started thinking that Pete appreciated me more than the staff I worked with. I was already dissatisfied in Kokomo, and I thought my situation would probably be better in Nashville. Pete's church was four times the size of the one I worked at. Bigger was better, I thought, and I could finally get the respect I deserved.

After about a month of talking to Pete behind Trisha's back,

I finally approached her and told her of our conversations. She wasn't happy. No, that's an understatement. She was *furious*. I told her I wasn't asking her to move—yet—because I didn't know whether God was in this possibility.

Within a few short weeks of my confession, I wore Trisha down to embracing the potential of moving. We would be at a bigger church. We would have more influence. We could do greater things for God's Kingdom. Starting all over would be hard, I reasoned, but it would be worth it. God could use us in more impressive ways.

It is so easy to equate following your own desires with pursuing God's will, and that is exactly what I'd done. In my thought process, I wanted to be noticed and respected more by leading a larger ministry. Because of this, I had moved my wife from a church that loved her, from friends she was attached to, and from a community we were invested in to a place without any of those things. And what was so damaging to our marriage was that I presented it all under the umbrella of God's will. My attitude had become, "I deserve this, so this must be God's will."

Shortly after moving to Nashville, we came to another crossroads. From the moment we arrived, we noticed there was turmoil and turnover on the staff of the church. Within a few months of our arrival, nine different staff members resigned. I remember standing in the auditorium on Sunday morning shortly after we moved and whispering to Trish, "I'm so sorry. We made the biggest mistake of our lives by moving here." She didn't say anything, but tears streamed down her face during worship.

Because of the conflict on our staff and the constant tension and transition I was dealing with, I became very disconnected at home. I didn't want to talk. I didn't want to invest. I felt numb—in our marriage and in my relationship with God. I didn't want to have to feel anything. Trisha had had all she could take.

Trisha came to me one evening and said, "I'm not doing well. I don't think you're doing well. I don't think our marriage is doing

well. I really think we need counseling. We've both been h͟
move, and I think we need help processing it and healing from͟

In my mind she was asking me to admit that we didn't have
it all together. But I was a pastor, and pastors should have it all
together. Pastors don't go to counseling; pastors *do* counseling.

"I know you're hurt," I said. "We'll get through this. I don't
think we need counseling. What is counseling going to do? *I* know
what the problem is. *You* know what the problem is. And besides,
we don't have the money for counseling." I ended the conversation.

My greatest fear was that counseling wouldn't help me; it would
expose me. We would go to counseling for what Trisha perceived to
be wrong with us, but the counselor would see right through me
and bring to light things that I didn't want to admit, didn't want to
deal with, didn't want Trisha to know about. So in one of the darkest
times of my life and one of the loneliest times in our marriage, I said
no to something that could have brought healing out of a fear that
it would bring more pain. The potential of that moment was lost.

TRISHA:

Six months into our time in Nashville, it was obvious that Justin
would need to look for another job. This time my heart was numb
and callous to what lay ahead. Although Nashville hadn't turned
out to be the dream job Justin had hoped for, I tried to believe
that God was still in control and that with every dark cloud, there
had to be a silver lining.

During our brief time in Nashville, Pete and Brandi became
dear friends. Pete was Justin's boss, and they spent a lot of time
reassuring and encouraging each other as the ministry grew harder
day by day. Brandi had just given birth to their first baby boy, and
she and I found solace in each other that we would survive this
whole mom thing! God used our friendship to encourage each
other and to remind us that God was not finished with us.

I don't think any of us realized the crossroads God was about to put in our path. The question was, would we choose the potential of the moment or allow it to pass us by?

The next few months brought Justin and me back together as a team, even though we didn't go to counseling. Beyond Pete and Brandi, we thankfully had our loving and supportive small group. As staff member after staff member turned in resignation letters, the church was no longer a place of community but rather a place of tension and heartache. Our small group was studying *Experiencing God*, by Henry Blackaby and Claude King. God used this book in a way that forever changed my life. Desperate to know what in the world God wanted from us, I read the author's words as God's speaking directly to my heart.

This book sparked renewed passion and desire in me to change the world through the local church. It also rekindled a passion for Justin and me to work together as a team. We started to dream again as we had when we were in college.

From the time we were dating, Justin and I had talked about starting a church. And after our time in Nashville, we were so disillusioned with corporate church that the idea of starting from scratch was appealing. God could use us to do church differently. And more than this, we didn't feel like Nashville was home. While we had built great friendships with Pete and Brandi, we missed Indiana.

We began to pray about planting a church somewhere in Indiana. Justin went to Indianapolis on Fridays, just driving around the city. He stayed with some friends in the Noblesville area, which was ten miles north of Indianapolis. He would call me and tell me about the growth in the area and the potential for what God could do there.

Within four short months, we put together a business plan and a timeline. Micah was finishing kindergarten, and as soon as school was out, we would move to Noblesville to start a church for people who didn't go to church. God had realigned our hearts with each other and with himself, and our boys were excited to be near family again. At the same time, Pete and Brandi decided to stay and plant a church in Nashville. This was the crossroads we had all prayed for. But for me, it meant leaving another set of friends I had grown to know and love.

JUSTIN:

When Trisha and I decided to start the church in Noblesville, I had this belief that things would get better because we were trusting God. We were being faithful. We were stepping out and living our faith in front of others. The potential we had to impact this world for Christ was huge. As we made plans to move, our marriage problems seemed to diminish. Focusing on the mission of the church we were starting and the challenges we would face allowed us to take our eyes off the problems we had with one another. We were a team again. Our issues and problems weren't resolved; they just became secondary to the task in front of us.

God's blessing isn't dependent on our spiritual, emotional, financial, or marital health. That was true in the life of Samson: God's presence and blessing, at least for most of his life, were with Samson despite his blatant sin and impulsive decisions. And it was definitely true for us as we prepared to plant Genesis Church in Noblesville. In many ways, this was the healthiest we had ever been as a couple. We were on the same page in our desire to plant the church; we had to trust in God in ways we never had before; we were finally living out our potential together. There was a sense that all we had was each other. We were in this together.

There is no doubt in my mind that planting the church was from God. There is also no doubt that planting the church medicated my discontentment. Being in charge, starting something from scratch, and beginning to realize my potential allowed my *see, want, get* mind-set to take over. What had been a liability in years past now felt like an asset and enabled this character flaw that plagued my heart to grow and blind me to the healing I desperately needed.

See. Want. Get.

TRISHA:

Our younger son, Elijah, had some major health issues that we were trying to figure out. At two and a half, he said only two words consistently: *ah ah*, which meant "momma," and *red*, which actually meant "red." He screamed the rest of the time. He screamed when he was happy and when he was mad. Since his birth, he had been hospitalized four times due to asthma. Just one week after Justin officially resigned from the Nashville church, we sold most of our possessions to prepare to move into a small, two-bedroom apartment in Indiana. We had only five thousand dollars to our name, and our medical insurance would be cut off in a matter of days. You can imagine the panic that went through my mind thinking we would be without coverage. The Saturday before we moved, Elijah had a major asthma attack, and I was just minutes from taking him to the hospital when his doctor called and said to meet him at his office. The doctor gave him a breathing treatment that he responded well to and sent us on our way with multiple prescriptions.

While waiting for his prescriptions at Walgreens, I felt an urge to purchase a pregnancy test. We were not trying to get pregnant, and the thought of being pregnant with no foreseen insurance in our future made me panic. But I bought the test anyway. Twenty minutes later, a positive sign appeared on the test, indicating that baby number three was on the way.

I remember calling Brandi in complete hysteria that we were pregnant, soon to be uninsured, and with two little boys, one of whom required expensive medication. Her response in the sweetest southern accent you can imagine was, "Can I be happy for you?"

As much as I appreciated her words, I longed to hear them from Justin. But I knew he would be just as panicked as I was. Obviously, I was grateful that God had blessed us with another baby, but I feared this news would jeopardize the team dynamic Justin and I had finally returned to. Three days later, with baby number three on the way, we moved to Noblesville, Indiana, to plant Genesis Church.

JUSTIN & TRISHA:

CHOICES DETERMINE DESTINATION

In his book *The Principle of the Path*, Andy Stanley says, "Our direction, not our intention, determines our destination."

We think we can overcome the direction we choose with the strength of our intentions. If we just intend to be better, we can ignore the force of the choices we've made in the past. But our consistent choices in a single direction determine our destination, not our intentions. That is why we've talked about spiritual warfare and oneness and truth telling and choosing a covenant relationship. Good intentions may be the enemy of realizing our potential in life and in our marriages because they can obscure the choices we've already made.

Samson probably didn't intend to break his Nazirite vow. But when he came to the crossroads of see, want, get, his intentions couldn't overcome the cumulative power of his direction, which had been set by the many smaller choices he'd made before.

We are, in many ways, a collection of our choices. The marriages we have today aren't reflections of the intentions we have; they are collections of the choices we have made. The choices that separate an ordinary marriage from an extraordinary marriage aren't usually earth shattering or huge. It is the small, mundane choices we make every day that cause the biggest difference.

POTENTIAL AT THE CROSSROADS

When you are trying to overcome an ordinary marriage by pursuing extraordinary, you will inevitably come to crossroads. You will have decisions to make that will determine the trajectory of your relationship with your spouse. Should you go to counseling or not? Should you quit your job because the environment is detrimental to your relationship with God, or should you stay because the money is good? Should you take a promotion that will require you to travel three days a week, or should you stay in your current position and eat dinner at home each night? Should you say yes to a full-time job when you feel called to be a stay-at-home mom?

The difference between ordinary and extraordinary isn't always as simple as what is wrong and right on the surface. The crossroads may be a decision between two "right" possibilities. But the difference between ordinary and extraordinary is found at the crossroads of selfishness and selflessness.

One of the most powerful Scriptures in all of the Bible is Philippians 2:3-8 (NIV):

Do nothing out of selfish ambition or vain conceit.
Rather, in humility value others above yourselves, not
looking to your own interests but each of you to the
interests of the others. In your relationships with one
another, have the same mindset as Christ Jesus:

Who, being in very nature God,
    did not consider equality with God something
        to be used to his own advantage;
rather, he made himself nothing
    by taking the very nature of a servant,
    being made in human likeness.
And being found in appearance as a man,
    he humbled himself
by becoming obedient to death—even death on a cross!

Paul says, "In your relationships with one another, have the same mindset as Christ Jesus." Jesus didn't just *intend* to be a servant, he *chose* to be a servant. He chose to put others (us) ahead of himself, even when this choice was painful for him (see Luke 22:41-44).

It doesn't take long for us as we read or watch the news to find a story of a gifted person with great influence taking the wrong fork at the crossroads, sacrificing his or her potential. Most of these stories involve that person choosing what was in their own best interest rather than what was in the best interest of others. It's easy for us to think, *What a stupid move! I would never do that.* The Bible is filled with stories that make us think similarly. If you take the time to read the story of Samson in Judges 13–16, you'll walk away with the same conclusion.

Samson was clearly gifted to do great things for God. He was chosen to rescue the Israelites from the Philistines. And even though Samson still did some amazing things and "the Spirit of the LORD came powerfully upon him" time after time—even in the midst of his bad choices—Samson is the poster boy for unrealized potential. Whereas many of the other heroes in the book of Judges ruled in Israel after their epic battles, keeping the Israelites on track with the Lord at least while they remained alive, Samson died prematurely, in one final burst of God's strength. Samson's failure to reach his potential didn't come about as a result of one big mistake that cost him everything. Samson continually came to smaller crossroads where he had to choose between what he wanted and what God wanted for him.

It was Samson's small, incremental choices to pursue his selfish desires that led to his eventually sacrificing his potential. We typically think of Samson's downfall being the cutting of his hair, but Samson had long before chosen to forsake his Nazirite vow. He had already intentionally touched something that was dead (Judges 14:8-9), and he had likely had alcoholic drinks as well (Judges 14:10). Samson's hair was probably the last thread connecting Samson to his Nazirite vow and God's intention for his life. Samson was not crushed in an instant by circumstances beyond his control but under the building weight of a lifetime of poor decisions.

The same thing is true for marriage. Most days, you won't be faced with large decisions that will incite your spouse to file for divorce. The crossroads that all of us stand at every day is do I choose ordinary again today, or do I choose extraordinary? Do I choose what I want, what I deserve, what my spouse owes me, what I've paid the price for—or do I choose what is best for my spouse and my marriage?

One thing I know is that you can't be selfish and have an extraordinary marriage. Marriage isn't designed for selfish people. Maybe you are reading this book right now and you are thinking, *I've been telling my husband that for years.* Another thing I know is that you can't be simultaneously selfless *and* resentful about your selflessness. Just as love is self-sacrificing, love also "keeps no record of being wronged" (1 Corinthians 13:5).

It is why this principle of the crossroads is so important. The choices we make every day determine the quality of our marriages. But more important than those choices are the heart and motivation with which we make them.

The selfish pattern of see, want, get will never bring you the marriage you long for. It will never bring you the relationship with God you desire. See, want, get will allow you to pursue your God-given dreams but will compromise your character along the way.

See, want, get always leads you and your marriage to a place of ordinary.

QUESTIONS

1. What potential did you see for your marriage while you and your spouse were still dating? What potential, if any, feels lost at this time in your life/marriage? Why is that so?

2. Is there a crossroads you are facing? What has been your process of deciding which path to take?

3. Samson's bad decisions incrementally destroyed his potential. Have you noticed this trend in your own life? If so, explain.

4. *See, want, get* was Samson's Achilles' heel. In what area of your life do you live out this pattern? What has been the result?

7

NO ORDINARY DEPENDENCE

WE MOVED to Noblesville, Indiana, on June 1, 2002, and on June 9, we had our very first core group meeting of Genesis Church. Nine people came, but from the energy in the room, it seemed as if one hundred were in attendance! What made this group even more special was that some people from the church in Kokomo—including my (Trisha's) best friend and her husband—decided they would give us a one-year commitment to help us start the church. We all felt a huge sense of anticipation for what God could do through this small but determined group.

God's blessing continued just a few months later as our family of four moved from an apartment to a four-bedroom house. Soon after, I gave birth to our sweet baby boy Isaiah. Meanwhile, our church was growing rapidly. All those earlier years of dreaming and fighting through disappointment now seemed worth it. It felt like we were finally realizing our potential. I loved my life and felt such excitement and passion for all God was doing and providing.

Even though our church was a small plant, God had gone before us. Our past marriage mistakes were truly behind us. Justin and I were doing this ministry together—as a team. Our church had potential. Our marriage had potential again. We had come to a crossroads in our marriage, and we had finally chosen the right path.

Or so we thought.

JUSTIN:

It didn't take long for us to realize that God's vision for the church we were starting was much bigger than our own. We moved to Noblesville with five thousand dollars and a sincere belief that we could have a church built to support us by the time we ran out of money. Keep in mind that this wasn't the 1800s, when five thousand dollars was a lot more than it sounds like. This was 2002, when five thousand dollars was more like . . . five thousand dollars. It was a lot of money in many respects, but not a large amount of money to support a family of four, soon to be five, and to start a church. But we went for it.

For the first few months of the church, we met at our apartment complex clubhouse and organized praise and worship with an overhead projector (we were cutting edge). Our "children's ministry" met in our apartment with a college girl we paid to watch the eight to ten kids who would come each week. We had two-way radios that served as our paging system if the kids needed their parents. It was a very humble beginning, but it was a blast. Trisha led worship each week, and I'd cast vision. The twelve to fifteen people would be so excited at the end of each of our gatherings. We all really believed that God was going to launch a movement through us. We were so dependent on him.

One morning, I showed up for a breakfast meeting that had been arranged by a guy I had tried to convince to lead worship for our church. He loved the church he attended and wasn't interested in leaving, but he wanted me to meet his pastor, Craig. I had no idea what to expect, but my assumption going into the meeting was that his pastor would not be thrilled that we were starting a church because many pastors see other churches as competition.

Craig shared his story of starting BridgeWay Community Church in Fishers, Indiana, just three years earlier. I knew immediately that our meeting was a God thing. When he had finished, he said, "So tell me the vision of Genesis Church." I gave him the business plan I had come up with, but we didn't open it in that meeting. I just shared my heart for our church, for the community, and for people who are far from God.

Tears streamed down Craig's face. He said, "We moved here with that same vision, and I want to help you however I can. I want my church to partner with you." I didn't know what to say. I was blown away.

Within a few weeks, Craig had introduced Trisha and me to the leaders of his church and had given me office space with his staff. God's favor continued in the church's relationship with Craig and BridgeWay, and Genesis Church moved our gatherings from Sunday nights at the apartment complex to BridgeWay on Sunday mornings.

BridgeWay had two Sunday morning services, and the church gave us meeting space during the nine o'clock service and provided our kids with childcare. Then our entire church—all twenty of us— would attend their eleven o'clock service together. Craig pointed us out each week and invited people from his church to join what God was calling us to do in Noblesville. It was something I'd never experienced in church before. Craig was so unselfish, so Kingdom minded. Over the next few months, God grew our church from twenty to fifty, and we were running out of space.

One of the things I learned about Craig was that he had moved to Noblesville five years before we had with a vision to plant a thriving, growing church in that community. God hadn't opened any doors for that church in Noblesville, so they moved to Fishers, just a few miles south of Noblesville. Craig and his wife, Lisa, like Trisha and me, had moved to the community not knowing anyone. Just as BridgeWay was adopting us, they had been adopted by Grace

Community Church, who had given them meeting space, offices, people, and resources. Craig introduced me to Dave Rodriguez, the senior pastor at Grace, and I set up a lunch appointment with him. Grace was the largest church on the north side of Indianapolis—and possibly the whole city—so I was a little intimidated.

When I sat down to meet with Dave, he said, "I hear you're running out of meeting space at BridgeWay. We'd like to offer you space here at Grace. Not only that, we want to give you as many people as you can take with you and some money to help with your launch."

I remember saying to Dave, "You know we're planting this church in Noblesville, right? We'll be less than three miles from your building. Are you sure you want to help us out like that?"

I'll never forget what he said to me in that moment: "Justin, I wouldn't care if you planted your church across the street from Grace. It is God who draws people to churches, not pastors. We want to help you because as we help you, we help the Kingdom."

On Mother's Day weekend 2003, we held our first Saturday night service in a Sunday school classroom at Grace Community Church. We had seventy-eight people there that night. God was definitely up to something big. That summer, Dave allowed me to speak at Grace's services one weekend in front of seven thousand people. At the end of the message, he came up and said to his congregation, "This fall, Genesis Church will launch public services, and some of you need to leave here and go with them." It was incredible. God was blessing. God was moving. God was watching over our church.

But as the church grew and the pressure of being a senior pastor set in, the church became my idol. Without fully realizing it, I began to worship the blessings of God more than I worshiped God himself. I started counting on the church, its attendance numbers, its success, and the feelings of significance and value it gave me more than I counted on God. It wasn't a sudden shift; it was subtle. The vision *God* had for our church had become an all-consuming vision that *I* had for our church. My life and marriage revolved not around God, but around the roles and responsibilities Trisha and I had at the church.

TRISHA:

By summer 2004, the church had grown to over five hundred people. Not only had our vision become a reality, but those who called Genesis their home took ownership of the vision. Parents were bringing their teenagers, wives were bringing their unsaved husbands, and we even had an elderly couple attending from a nearby nursing home. We were preparing for a capital campaign that would allow us to purchase the Arbortorium banquet hall (the "Arb"), which we rented each week for Sunday services. It was a sweet time in the church's history.

But where there is growth, change is always soon to follow. As the church grew, so did our need for leaders. That July we had our first leaders' retreat. About twenty leaders attended, and for me, it was the first time in the history of being in ministry that I felt out of place. What should have been an extraordinary moment in the life of our church was for me lonely, confusing, and frustrating—not exactly the emotions you'd expect to flow from a heart that was being blessed with so much.

I sat in the back watching the leaders in the room soak in the vision Justin was casting. As he talked, I wondered, *Why doesn't he notice me sitting here? Why isn't he fighting for me?* I was jealous of the intimate relationship he seemed to have with his church but not with me. I was angry over all I had sacrificed for these leaders and my husband to even *have* this church to lead. I felt that the church had become more like a mistress than the bride of Christ. The church was my competition, fighting for Justin's time, attention, and affection.

In that moment I felt God tell me to confess to Justin and my close friends how I was feeling. I could sense his gentle whisper encouraging me not to give up but to stand firm in him and fight—fight for the extraordinary relationship that was only possible through him. But I ignored God's plea. Not wanting to create conflict, I said nothing. By not sharing my struggles, I allowed my heart to wander down a dark path where my jealousy grew into a cancer of resentment that began to slowly kill our marriage.

JUSTIN:

In the spring of 2004, Trisha and a team of volunteers went to Willow Creek Community Church in Chicago for an arts conference. She was going to be gone for a few days, and that left me home with our eight-year-old, five-year-old, and almost-one-year-old. Our boys are good kids, but me plus them for two days equaled stress fest.

About halfway through day two, I decided I was going to make frozen pizza for lunch. There was no way I could mess that up. I put the pizza in the oven, set the timer, and got the kids downstairs and ready to eat. As I opened the oven to pull the pizza out, our youngest son, Isaiah, was right at my feet. I tripped over him, and he lost his balance, falling forward into the open oven. Trying to brace his fall, he put his hands on the open oven door.

Instantly I heard skin burning. He cried as blisters appeared, and I frantically ran his hands under cold water. I called Trisha to see how close she was to the house. Isaiah was screaming in the background as I tried to explain to her what had happened and that I needed her to get home as soon as possible. My makeshift bandages would have to suffice until she arrived. I had an elders' meeting that night, the kids were stressing me out, and I'd had about all I could take. Trisha told me they were just leaving Willow Creek and that she would be home in three hours. That was about two hours and forty-five minutes longer than I wanted, but I couldn't change anything.

Two hours later I called to see how close they were. Trisha told me they were stuck in traffic just outside Chicago and hadn't moved in over an hour. I went nuts. How in the world could she let herself get stuck in traffic? Didn't she realize how stressed I was? Didn't she know I had a meeting in a few hours that I couldn't be late for? How dare she do this to me!

Another two hours passed, and it was time for supper. I wasn't going to take any chances cooking, so we went to McDonald's. On the way home, Isaiah puked in his car seat, which would have been manageable except for one detail.

I'm a sympathetic puker.

So as I raced home, the car filled with the unhappy smell of a vomited Happy Meal. I began to gag, and waves of nausea washed over me. Struggling to hold it in, I screeched into the driveway and leapt into the fresh air. I was so furious at Trisha by this point that I refused to clean up the puke. I yanked out the car seat with puke all over it and sat it in the middle of the driveway.

About thirty minutes later, Trisha pulled up to the house.

I was mere minutes away from being late for my meeting. I met her in the driveway, handed her my puke-smelling, hand-blistered son, and drove to my elder's meeting—to talk about how to lead our church spiritually.

In my mind, everything that day was her fault. She did it all on purpose. She got caught in traffic. She made me late for my meeting. She forced me to cook and then to avoid cooking. It was her fault things weren't extraordinary.

This attitude and behavior had moved from being the exception to the norm. Trisha was high maintenance. She was holding me back from ministry. She was at fault for just about everything. Our relationship wasn't necessarily volatile, but it was passive-aggressive. She would be mean, and I would heap on guilt and shame. We each had our ways of making the other pay, and it was eating our relationship alive.

TRISHA:

If you had been a fly on the wall in our house, you wouldn't have heard crashing dishes or loud arguments. It was in the small things that Justin and I tried to hurt each other. I would withhold physical intimacy. You don't come home when you said you would? You don't meet my expectations? You're on shutdown. It was one area I knew would hurt Justin. But I had no idea the fire I was messing with in this whole area of our relationship.

My new goal was to force Justin to make up to me for all the times he moved me. To make up for the fact that the only reason he had his church was because of *my* willingness to live sacrificially. To make up for using me to start this church and then pushing me to the side when I was no longer needed. I was placing godlike expectations on Justin to fill a void in my life that I felt he was responsible for causing in the first place. Justin became my idol: I was looking to him to give me what only God could give. Because God never designed Justin to fill that void in my life, he failed at it no matter when he did or didn't try.

But there was still a church that needed our attention, and in order for Justin to continue leading it, we needed to stay married. My partnership with Justin was now reduced to stepping into areas of ministry where he was desperate for a leader and taking care of our home and kids. Our once-extraordinary dream of changing the world *together* was coming to an end. We spent the next year learning to accept our marriage for what it now was: ordinary.

In the summer of 2005, we celebrated our tenth wedding anniversary. We had always wanted to go on a cruise to celebrate an anniversary, and now more than ever, we needed time alone. In the back of my mind, I hoped some time alone with Justin would allow us to rediscover some of the passion that had cooled over the years. For the first time since Micah's birth, it was just the two of us. For those four days, we went without e-mail, cell phones, parenting duties, and ministry issues. And in those four days, I fell in love with Justin all over again. Extraordinary still had a chance! All the distractions of life that seemed to bring out the worst in us were gone. It was just us, and I loved every minute.

When the cruise ended, we had some time to kill before leaving for the airport. As we sat down for lunch, before we could even order our food, Justin's phone rang. He answered it without skipping a beat. We hadn't even been off the boat an hour, and someone else was already calling for his attention. All the peace and perfection of our four days together melted into a puddle at my feet. Our glimpse of something new was just that. It had been merely a brief break from ordinary.

I cried softly, and when Justin finally hung up, my cries became heart-wrenching sobs.

"I don't want to go back!" I told him.

I didn't want to go back to ministry. I didn't want to go back to the breakneck pace. I didn't want to go back to being invisible.

But I knew we didn't have a choice. I was in love with my husband, yet I knew that the battleground we were returning to would not cultivate our relationship like a cruise ship in the middle of the ocean. I knew life was about to get hard again, but never in my wildest dreams did I expect us to drift as far and as fast as we did in the days to come.

JUSTIN:

A few weeks after the cruise, I got a call on a Sunday afternoon from someone on our board of directors at the church. Not only was he on our board, he was also one of my closest friends and advisers. I respected him, and I trusted him even more than I trusted myself.

He asked me if we could ride four-wheelers together. I'm not an outdoorsman at all—I don't fish or hunt or camp—so his invitation meant a lot to me because he enjoyed all of those things. I said I'd love to ride four-wheelers through the woods!

About halfway through our ride, we stopped for a few minutes next to a creek and started throwing rocks into the water. In what I know was a God moment, he shared with me some things that were on his heart and some things that were happening in his marriage, and he asked my advice. These things weren't ground-breaking or earth-shattering confessions, but he was vulnerable. I wasn't just his pastor; I was his friend.

I stood on the side of a creek, but I also stood at a crossroads. I felt a prompting from the Holy Spirit: *You can tell him. He's safe. You can tell him of the problems you have—the issues you and Trisha are going through.* At the same time, another voice said, *He's your biggest contributor. He's a member of your board. At best he will leave the church and take his money and influence with him; at worst he will have you fired, and it will cost you this friendship.*

I chose to stay hidden. I chose not to come clean about the dysfunction in my marriage, about the sin I had allowed to creep into my heart, about some choices I was contemplating.

In my mind, confession would cost me something. Confession would put me at risk. Confession would be the end of my ministry. Confession would jeopardize what he thought of me.

Not confessing in that moment proved to be one of the biggest mistakes of my life.

TRISHA:

JOURNAL ENTRY—AUGUST 25, 2005

Wow, Lord, I can't believe what a manic person I am at times. What is my deal? Father, I ask that you would forgive me and give me clean hands and a pure heart toward the people I love and know that you love. I'm trying so hard to give up my chains, but I feel like I will always carry them. I don't want them to shape who I am. Help me to slow down. It is so rough around here at times. I don't want to be in ministry anymore! Please help me to have a spirit of calmness and love. In my heart I am at such odds with Justin and my best friend that it makes me sick to think about. How can I be at odds with two of the people I love the most, yet I have no idea why I feel this way? What has changed? I don't know how to protect my heart anymore. It makes me so raw with emotion that I don't even know what to do with it. I know that you know everything, so please give me the wisdom and discernment to figure it all out. I can't stay at this place emotionally or bounce back and forth from happy to feeling angry, but those are the manic emotions I keep feeling. I want that link of my chain to come off. I know that I am nothing without you. Embed that into my heart.

The following Sunday, I went to an elder and his wife between our Sunday services and completely broke down. I told them I was struggling and that Justin and I were at a very dangerous and dark place in our marriage. Relieved I had finally come clean, my tears turned into soft quivers like those of a two-year-old who has just gotten over a good cry. But that relief was quickly replaced with disbelief. They told me that they were sorry, but in the end they patted me on the back as if to say I was overreacting. To me it communicated that they thought I was crazy. Satan tormented me with that possibility for the next three weeks.

I knew that Jesus would help me; I just wanted him to help me in the way I thought he should. Justin and I were no longer fighting as enemies. It was worse: we fought as strangers. We became so blinded by our own sin and personal struggles that it seemed impossible to repair the damage we inflicted on each other. Just weeks after the cruise, it became more and more evident that Justin didn't want to spend time with me, and in the process, I completely shut down. Our relationship had taken a dangerous turn when I realized that Justin no longer cared about how I thought or felt about him. He was tired of pretending, and I just went numb.

If our leaders' retreat in 2004 was a huge achievement, going to Catalyst should have been even bigger. Catalyst is a next-generation leaders' conference that Justin had been going to since it first began in 1999. In 2005, we were not only bringing volunteers with us to Catalyst, we were bringing staff! The richness God had blessed both Justin and me with should have left us smiling from ear to ear. But instead this conference marked my life in a way I could have never imagined.

The focus of the conference was on character and integrity. Bill Hybels, whom Justin had looked up to for years, gave a powerful message that was prophetic for the dark turn our marriage was about to take. Halfway through another speaker's message, Justin and our good friend Pete (who was also there with his staff) disappeared. When they returned, I could tell by the look on Pete's face that things were not right.

I've watched shows like *48 Hours Mystery* and find myself talking to the screen as if the people can hear me. I say things like, "How could he *not* have known . . . ?" or "Why on earth didn't she run?" It's easy to forget that TV gives us a panoramic view of the story rather than placing us in the middle of it. Still, I *knew* something was wrong at Catalyst. I knew there was a storm on the horizon. I had no clue what made up that storm; I just knew I needed to prepare for it.

So when we returned from the conference, I prepared in the only way I knew how: I dropped a hundred dollars we didn't have on a new outfit. I painted my nails. I woke up really early to make myself look the best I could. I was praying I was beautiful enough that Justin would notice me in hopes that he would want to rescue me from the storm that was about to hit. Never did I anticipate that Jesus would have to be the one to rescue us both.

JUSTIN & TRISHA:

If you read through the Old Testament, you will see a pattern emerge in the nation of Israel. God blessed them, and Israel would worship him. Then their attention would become divided, and the Bible says in a number of different places that the Israelites did what was evil in the eyes of the Lord. This usually refers to the propensity the Israelites had to worship other gods. They would give to idols and false gods the affection of their hearts. God would allow other nations and kingdoms to conquer his people, and as they experienced heartache, hardship, and defeat, they would cry out to God, and he would rescue them.

In 2 Kings 17, the northern kingdom of Israel is conquered by the Assyrians. Israel is exiled out of the Promised Land, and the Assyrians move other exiles to Samaria—the northern kingdom's capital—to take their place. These transplanted exiles start worshiping other gods. God doesn't like their worship of idols, so he sends lions to attack and maul people. Parenthetically, that is just cool! He could have chosen lightning, fire, or flood, but he specifically chooses lions. Epic!

The king of Assyria realizes that something isn't right and figures out that his people are being attacked by God because of their idol worship. So he sends some exiled priests of Israel back to Samaria to teach the newly resettled foreigners how to worship God. Think of it—he wants the Israelite priests to evangelize these subjects of Assyria! Here's what happens:

> These new residents worshiped the LORD, but they also
> appointed from among themselves all sorts of people
> as priests to offer sacrifices at their places of worship.
> And though they worshiped the LORD, they continued
> to follow their own gods according to the religious
> customs of the nations from which they came. And this
> is still going on today. They continue to follow their
> former practices instead of truly worshiping the LORD
> and obeying the decrees, regulations, instructions, and
> commands he gave the descendants of Jacob, whose name
> he changed to Israel. . . . So while these new residents
> worshiped the LORD, they also worshiped their idols.
> And to this day their descendants do the same.
> 2 KINGS 17:32-34, 41

"They also worshiped their idols." It's not that they didn't say the prayers or sing the songs or go to the services. They were cool with God. They were happy to worship him—they didn't want to get mauled by lions anymore. But they also worshiped their idols.

"THEY ALSO . . ."

Ordinary marriages live in the world of "they also."

Idol worship isn't something that comes at us all of a sudden. It's something that drifts slowly into our lives. What makes it so dangerous is that it's not like God doesn't have a role in our lives. He does. But he isn't where we find our value. He isn't where we find our contentment. He isn't where we find our self-esteem. He isn't where we find our identity. And often without even realizing it, we look to something else—our jobs, our possessions, our homes, even our marriages—to give us what only God can give. With that subtle shift, we put a lid on our ability to go beyond ordinary in our relationships with God or with our spouses.

What is very interesting is this pattern continued throughout the Old Testament with the nation of Israel. They would find success and initially worship God. Then they would take their eyes off of God and start to worship idols, build Asherah poles, and make pagan shrines. God would allow them to be conquered, captured, or exiled, and the people would cry out to God to deliver them. This pattern continued until the time of Nehemiah.

Initially, this scenario looked similar, but in the events of the book of Nehemiah, everything changed:

> In late autumn, in the month of Kislev, in the twentieth
> year of King Artaxerxes' reign, I was at the fortress of
> Susa. Hanani, one of my brothers, came to visit me with
> some other men who had just arrived from Judah. I asked
> them about the Jews who had returned there from
> captivity and about how things were going in Jerusalem.

They said to me, "Things are not going well for those who returned to the province of Judah. They are in great trouble and disgrace. The wall of Jerusalem has been torn down, and the gates have been destroyed by fire."

When I heard this, I sat down and wept. In fact, for days I mourned, fasted, and prayed to the God of heaven. Then I said,

"O LORD, God of heaven, the great and awesome God who keeps his covenant of unfailing love with those who love him and obey his commands, listen to my prayer! Look down and see me praying night and day for your people Israel. I confess that we have sinned against you. Yes, even my own family and I have sinned! We have sinned terribly by not obeying the commands, decrees, and regulations that you gave us through your servant Moses.

"Please remember what you told your servant Moses: 'If you are unfaithful to me, I will scatter you among the nations. But if you return to me and obey my commands and live by them, then even if you are exiled to the ends of the earth, I will bring you back to the place I have chosen for my name to be honored.'

"The people you rescued by your great power and strong hand are your servants. O Lord, please hear my prayer! Listen to the prayers of those of us who delight in honoring you. Please grant me success today by making the king favorable to me. Put it into his heart to be kind to me."

NEHEMIAH 1:1-11

The capital city was in ruins. The wall of Jerusalem was torn down. The city gates were destroyed by fire. The people of Israel had been stripped of everything that represented God's provision, blessing, and presence. So often in our own lives, God will strip us of everything we use to find security, identity, and value so he can reattach us to himself. His greatest desire is that we depend on him.

In this passage, Nehemiah doesn't just rescue the people of Israel like the Old Testament heroes did in the past; he repents on behalf of the people. He asks God to forgive them. He begs God to realign their hearts with his.

Remarkably, after this point in the Old Testament, God's people struggled much less with idol worship. Once the wall was rebuilt, so was their faith and dependence on God.

Have you been to that place in your life or in your marriage? If you haven't yet, the odds are you will arrive there at some point. You didn't know how you were going to make it. You had no clue how that bill was going to be paid. You had no idea whether you would recover from that illness. You didn't know if you would be able to buy that house. You had no sense of how you and your spouse would get through such a difficult time or recover from such a painful mistake. When our circumstances grow beyond our ability to control them, we turn to God to do what only he can do.

God will use circumstances, heartache, stress, or failure to grow our dependence on him. If we don't allow him that space in our life, if we live with a "they also" faith, then often we find ourselves in a place of hurt, destruction, devastation, and ruin. It's in those moments when we realize that we are not as much in control as we thought. Our reliance on God increases as our ability to control things decreases.

That was where God was taking our church and our marriage. Although at the time we didn't realize it, God was preparing to use destruction and hurt in our lives to realign our hearts with his.

Sometimes going beyond ordinary requires more than you think you can give—and requires more dependence on God than you think you can have.

QUESTIONS

1. What are some situations that have caused you to depend on God in your marriage? What has been the outcome of that dependence?

2. When you're not on the same page with your spouse, are you tempted to withhold truth? If so, what prompts you to do this? Why?

3. Do you feel pressure to make up for mistakes made in your marriage? Why or why not?

4. How have you seen the idea of "they also" apply to your life or marriage? Have you been brought through this "they also" season? If so, how? If not, how might you be?

8.

NO ORDINARY CONFESSION

OCTOBER 9, 2005, the day after we returned from Catalyst, Trisha had just led worship at church and I (Justin) had just spoken about the importance of godly relationships. Now back at home, Trisha was upstairs in our bedroom getting ready to take a nap. Our kids were downstairs watching TV. It seemed like a typical Sunday afternoon.

I sat down on our bed. "Trisha, we need to talk."

"What is it?" she said.

"Trisha, I can't keep this from you anymore. I'm having an affair. I'm having an affair with your best friend. I don't love you. I don't want to be married to you. I want out."

It wasn't a confession of remorse, regret, or repentance. It was a confession of resignation. I was finished.

Trisha left the house in a hysterical panic, but I was cold, calculated. A few minutes later, one of the elders of our church called. Trisha must have called him as soon as she pulled out of the driveway.

I asked him to call the other elders together and meet at my house. It wasn't long before they arrived, and I had already printed out my resignation letter. I had cheated on them, too, made worse by the fact that Trisha's best friend was the children's director at church.

I wanted out of all of it. I was as done with ministry as I was with my marriage. Despite the elders' words of admonition, despite their pleading to give my marriage a chance, I wanted out.

It was over.

TRISHA:

With Justin's confession:
I lost my church family.
I lost my best friend.
I lost my husband.
I lost my identity.
I lost everything.

JOURNAL ENTRY—OCTOBER 11, 2005

Father, I feel as if there are no words that describe the depth of my pain. I love Justin with all my heart and soul. I want him back so badly, but I have realized he is not the person right now that I thought he was. I am still angry with you! I know that Justin chose sin; I just don't understand why you didn't send anyone to save or protect him. I am trying so hard to be strong. I am so thankful for my amazing family and friends. You mean the world to me. I want to continue to follow your will for my life, whether that's with or without Justin. But I need you to guide me! I need the Holy Spirit to guide this situation because I cannot in my own will or power. Please heal Justin's heart and let him know you love him even more. Help me to know when he is lying and when he's deceiving. Help me to be what you need me to be. Lastly,

Father, I beg you—please give me the right words to say to my boys. Please allow the Holy Spirit to speak your truth in a way they will understand. I love you, Lord, and I know you will use this to bring glory to your name. God, please, please, please give me the strength to do so.

The following week became a crossroads of choosing to lean into God in every moment, not just the ones I thought he should be a part of. Life was going to be different—that was clear—but I had to choose if I would continue to live as I always had or if I would allow God to break me and trust that he is who he said he is. I would have to make painful decisions either way, with some of them being made after different pieces of the puzzle came together. The bigger question for me was, would I be willing to choose redemption even when it would cost me something more, after already paying such a high price?

JUSTIN:

I had resigned from our church and left my wife and three boys. My plan was to pursue the relationship with Trisha's best friend. My church office was cleaned out. My mind was made up. I wanted to leave my ordinary marriage and have an extraordinary relationship with this other woman. I checked into a hotel just down the street from our church and planned on moving forward in that direction.

Trisha called me the night of my confession and begged me to come home. She loved me and wanted to do anything she could to make our marriage work. I was convinced it couldn't be fixed. I had messed up too bad. I had gone too far. I had hurt her beyond repair. Our marriage was beyond redemption.

She asked me, "Do you love me?"

"Yes," I said.

"Are you in love with me?"

"No, I'm not in love with you."

Her voice shook. "Are you in love with my best friend?"

"Yes."

That was the last time I heard Trisha's voice for the next fifteen days. Later that night, I got a phone call from a church member who was with Trisha. She told me that if I had any hope at all of restoring our marriage, I needed to show up at a counseling appointment she had made for me the following morning.

Now that I had resigned from the church, I had nothing else to do, so I went to the appointment. I shared with the counselor what had taken place the day before. She asked me a question I didn't expect. "What do you want to accomplish through this counseling session? What are your expectations?"

I was done hiding. I was done pretending. It was time to be honest. "I want you to help me figure out how God is going to bless me no matter who I choose. If I stay in this marriage or if I choose to pursue the other relationship, I want God to bless me."

The counselor told me she couldn't help me. I was on my own.

I left the counseling session feeling liberated. I wasn't saying what I should say anymore; I said what I felt. I wasn't doing what other people thought I should do anymore. I was doing what I wanted to do—what I *deserved* to do.

I left Noblesville for my parents' house. I had called my parents to tell them what was going on, and I asked that they gather my brothers and sister so I could inform them of my decision. My parents had been separated for different lengths of time when I was growing up. My sister was divorced and remarried. My youngest brother was divorced and dating again. My other brother was married to a divorced woman. If I were to have a cheering section, my family would be it. They would understand where I was coming from.

I arrived at my parents' house and could tell things weren't going to go as I had envisioned. There were no hugs. There were no sympathetic *I'm sorrys*. There was only hurt. There was only disappointment. One of my brothers asked why I would throw my life away. The other told me that everything he respected about me and my relationship with God was over. My sister said, "What will your boys think of you when you tell them that you want to marry someone other than their mom? What kind of legacy is that?" I'm sure there was a lot more said, but those were the words that punctured the armor I had built around my heart over the past few months.

I wanted to go home.

I got in my car, determined to fight for my family. I wanted to fight for Trish. I wanted to fight for my kids. I was sorry. I called my friend Tom and told him I was coming home. He told me he would let Trisha know.

When I arrived home, my mother-in-law and the board member by the creek were waiting for me. I ran past them and into the garage, where Trisha was standing with another lady from our church. I fell at her feet and begged her to take me back. It was immediately obvious that my begging wasn't going to solve anything. My mother-in-law informed me that the choice to come home wasn't mine to make anymore. That window had closed. Trisha didn't want to see me. She didn't want to talk to me. She didn't want me at the house. She wasn't sure she wanted me back. With that, Trisha walked back into that house.

For the first time, my choices had consequences. I didn't realize the depth of those consequences at this point, but I realized that the control and manipulation I had worked to sustain for the past ten years were gone. I wasn't in control of this situation. I wasn't welcome to stay at the house. I had nowhere to go, so I went back to the hotel—alone. God seemed as unapproachable as Trisha.

I'm not one to overspiritualize everything. Up to this point in my life, I believed in spiritual warfare, I just didn't take it very seriously. But on this night in my hotel room, I felt a demonic presence unlike I had ever felt before. I don't remember everything that happened that night, but I remember screaming as loud as I could, "Satan, get out of here! Get out of here! Jesus, meet me right now! Jesus, save me from this darkness! I invite you, Jesus, into this room. I invite you into my heart again, Jesus. Jesus, help!"

I woke up the next morning lying next to my bed. I felt the first burst of repentance. I felt sorry for my sin and not just for the consequences of my sin. For the first time in a long time, I saw how far I had drifted from God and from my wife. The weight of the choices I had made crashed on me.

How did I get here? How did I allow my relationship with God and Trisha to become so inauthentic and broken? I had more questions than answers, but simply asking the questions seemed like a good first step.

A few hours after I woke up, a friend from our church came to my hotel room. Tony and his wife, Suzy, had been our friends for a long time and had helped us start the church three years before. We drove to the park and talked. He was so disappointed and hurt. He had so many questions, and I had very few answers. There is really no way to justify sin; all I could do was ask for his forgiveness. Tony and Suzy extended to me the first of many acts of grace.

Tony said he had talked to Trisha and wanted to offer me a place to stay until we either divorced or put the pieces back together. He told me that Trisha would no longer be taking my calls. She didn't want me to text or e-mail her. She was requiring me to work through a mediator to communicate with her and to see our boys. He said to me, "You have messed your life and your ministry and your marriage up bad. But this woman loves you. She loves you so much. You need to figure out how you allowed yourself to get so broken." I wanted to know the answer to that too. I agreed to stay with Tony and Suzy.

When we walked into Tony's house, he said to me, "It's going to feel like it's over, but it's not over." I had no idea what that meant, but I soon found out. As we walked upstairs, he explained to me that I would be sleeping in his seven-year-old daughter's room. They had moved her stuff into her sister's room, and I could stay as long as I needed. In my mind, that wouldn't be more than a few days.

I walked into her room, and it felt like it was over. Everything I owned was stacked in boxes against the wall. Every shirt. Every pair of pants. Every pair of shoes. Every jacket. Every pair of socks and underwear. Everything. I fell to my knees, and the gravity of my choices overwhelmed me.

The next day, I went back to the counselor's office. I was desperate to make things right. I was broken. I was sorry. I desperately wanted a second chance. The distance between Trisha and me was immense. The mountain we had to climb seemed insurmountable. Beyond my marriage, I felt like I was starting over in my relationship with God. I had hurt him, too. I had taken advantage of grace. I had squandered my gifts and my position, and I had no idea where to start, but I was committed to figuring it out.

In my heart, I had hope—for my marriage and for my relationship with God.

TRISHA:

It wasn't my idea to kick Justin out. I wanted him home, but he wanted out of our marriage.

On Monday afternoon, I talked to a counselor on the phone, and what he said forever changed the direction of my life. He said, "Until you let Justin go, you will be his scapegoat for all of his issues. If you stop trying to fix him and start telling him it's okay, he will continue on this path. And what he's done is not okay. Justin needs to seek God first, not you. He needs to believe that if he allows God to bring him to a place of brokenness and if you allow God to bring you to a place of brokenness, then your natural response will be to choose each other."

My first thought was, *This guy is an idiot and shouldn't be counseling!* I replied, "But if I let him go, he will only choose her!"

His response was deafening: "He already has."

I hung up the phone, and with my mom and my sweet friend Shelly by my side, I went up to our bedroom and started packing Justin's stuff. I smelled every piece of clothing I folded. I sobbed when I placed the last shirt in the packing tub. It was like he was dead, but he wasn't. In fact, it was *worse* than death. Justin was alive, but didn't choose me.

You can imagine the shock on my face when just hours after packing Justin's clothes, our friend Tom called and told my mom that Justin was on his way to the house! Sheer panic came over me. Before I could respond, Justin pulled into the driveway with Tom following close behind. It was like time stopped. I met Justin in the garage, where he fell to my feet sobbing and saying, "I'm sorry!" over and over again.

Everything in me wanted to hold him, but anger took over. I screamed for him to leave. I have never shared this part of our story before because it's so painful even to think about. But this event was my first step onto the narrow path. I could no longer be a shortcut for Justin. He needed to find his own path of broken-ness. The narrow path meant I no longer could ignore my own issues in order to deal with his. My new journey had begun, and I was scared to death of what God would uncover.

I chose not to talk to Justin for the next fifteen days, not because I was punishing him, but because I knew that if I was going to embrace change, I couldn't allow myself to try to help him. Those next fifteen days were some of the hardest yet most intimate days with God.

JUSTIN & TRISHA:

COPING MECHANISMS

I think the hardest part about sin is that each of us has a coping mechanism we use to deal with it. Some of us overeat, some of us stuff our emotions, while others retreat or stay in denial. Whatever our coping mechanisms happen to be, we use them to keep ourselves from having to confront our painful situations head on. I (Trisha) had been asking God for help in my prayers, but I wasn't allowing him to transform me. The price was too high, and it was easier to hide behind my method of coping with the situation—

being mean—than it was to take the narrower and more costly path of facing what was happening.

James describes our tendency to simultaneously ask God for help and use coping mechanisms as being "double-minded":

> If any of you lacks wisdom, you should ask God, who gives generously to all without finding fault, and it will be given to you. But when you ask, you must believe and not doubt, because the one who doubts is like a wave of the sea, blown and tossed by the wind. That person should not expect to receive anything from the Lord. Such a person is double-minded and unstable in all they do.
>
> JAMES 1:5-8, NIV

Double-mindedness keeps us from the help we desire: full healing and reconciliation. Instead, double-mindedness sets our desires against God's, proving futile for us since we're asking for God's help in the first place! Our coping mechanisms, our attempts to avoid pain in our own strength, are counter to the kind of healing God wants to provide and even cause the instability we try to avoid. Instead, we are to view the trials we face as "an opportunity for great joy" because these trials develop perseverance and maturity (James 1:2-4). God's desire for us, as it was for the Israelites in the desert, is to refine us.

But the process of refinement is painful, and when we ask God for help, we are often looking for an easy solution rather than the help we truly need. James later adds to this point: "You don't have what you want because you don't ask God for it. And even when you ask, you don't get it because your motives are all wrong—you want only what will give you pleasure" (James 4:2-3). When we desire to avoid pain more than we desire intimacy, ordinary is the only result we can expect.

THE PATH OF RESENTMENT

The problem with our coping mechanisms is that by using them we are not dealing with our pain. This pain then festers and puts us on the path of resentment, and resentment inevitably leads us away from our goal of true healing through reconciliation. Resentment is a silent assassin in marriage. Resentment is the author of ordinary, and it infects every aspect of our marriages. We cannot harbor bitterness in our hearts and love our spouses in an extraordinary way. Resentment kills the seed of love. And unfortunately, we often don't recognize resentment until it is too late.

Resentment has a way of disguising itself as self-protection. We put up walls of bitterness that we think will keep us from getting hurt again. But bitterness and resentment only produce unforgiveness. When we refuse to extend grace and forgiveness to our spouses, we undermine the self-protection we seek. In harboring bitterness toward our spouses and refusing to forgive them, we are refusing to allow God to heal and transform us.

There is an irony in Christians' struggle with forgiveness. As believers in Jesus, we have been saved by grace. We have been offered forgiveness. When we least deserved it, God forgave us. Yet many of us fail to forgive our friends, parents, siblings, coworkers, and yes, even our spouses.

Hurts, disappointments, wounds, resentment. You have accumulated them over the years. From your childhood, from college, now from your marriage. The person you love the most is the one who hurts you most often. Maybe not in big ways, but in consistent ways. These open wounds are eating away at you, robbing your marriage of the freedom that comes through forgiveness.

Resentment is easy; forgiveness is difficult. Our marriages put us in situations where we must decide over and over again whether to choose resentment or forgiveness. You will have opportunities to pursue and experience intimacy through forgiveness, but as we've mentioned, intimacy comes with a price. Grace is free but never ever cheap. There is always a price to redemption, and that cost is paid through gut-level honesty and refining. As with the principle of the Dip, it's so easy to stop just short of our moment of redemption because the path seems too difficult or painful. But the path of brokenness is the way to redemption, and there are no shortcuts.

THE PATH OF BROKENNESS

You may feel like your relationship with your spouse is nearing death. Starting on the journey toward reconciliation may seem hopeless, especially when the path is rocky. We have witnessed many people give up and step off the path rather than staying on it and finding healing. The truth is that this path is painful, narrow, and rugged. But it's a path that, should you choose to take it, will lead you to freedom and a new life found in God.

In the book of Job, we find a man on a path he didn't choose; it was chosen for him. In fact, the Bible says that Job "was blameless—a man of complete integrity" (Job 1:1). But God leads him to a narrow path that eventually costs him everything. His family, friends, and livelihood are taken from him in a painful turn of events. He questions. He argues. He pleads. But Job never stops dialoguing with God. He's bound and determined, even in his pit of despair, to figure out why God has placed him on this path, and he later comes to this conclusion:

> He knows where I am going.
>   And when he tests me, I will come out as pure as gold.
> For I have stayed on God's paths;
>   I have followed his ways and not turned aside.
> I have not departed from his commands,
>   but have treasured his words more than daily food.
> JOB 23:10-12

Although Job's circumstances brought about gut-wrenching pain, they didn't inherently bring brokenness. He had to choose it. Job was at a painful crossroads to daily choose brokenness over bitterness. Brokenness allowed Job to see past his circumstances and to treasure God's words more than even his daily food.

Brokenness is an act of surrender. It's giving up rather than just trying harder. Brokenness is a decision, laying everything on the line and then submitting it all to God. It is an awareness that God is your only hope. You can choose brokenness. The Bible says that God "will not reject a broken and repentant heart" (Psalm 51:17). He longs to see us desire brokenness, for it is in our brokenness and weakness that his strength is made perfect (2 Corinthians 12:9).

THE BENEFITS OF BROKENNESS

When we embrace brokenness, we can expect these benefits:

- *We lose our need to control.* When we have a faulty trust in God, we don't think he can control our lives as well as we can, so we manipulate. When we choose brokenness and surrender, we trust that God is in control, and we submit to what he desires and chooses. There's freedom in knowing he's in control.
- *We lose our need to impress.* When we choose brokenness, we lose our need to impress others. We begin to live out of an identity that isn't based on others' opinions, validations, or acceptance. When we live *only* trying to impress God, we discover a confidence and freedom that we've often tried to provide for ourselves but never could.
- *We lose our desire to pretend.* When we embrace brokenness, we stop pretending. We stop pretending we've got it all together, we've got all the answers, we have the perfect marriages and have overcome all sins. We lose our desire to pretend to be better friends, husbands, or parents than we

really are, and we desire to be more of who God calls us to be. We actually want to wake up and *be* the people we've been pretending to be, realizing that brokenness is the only way to get there.

- *We lose our need to hide.* As we find and embrace brokenness, our need to hide fades away, and all we are left with is *freedom*.

So how do you find this path? Do you have to sin to get there? Do you have to experience devastation to get there? The answer is no. Confession is necessary, but brokenness is available to anyone willing to pursue it. The truth, however, is that this path is most apparent in desperate situations because they come from a place of crisis. Most of us don't choose this path, because there's nothing appealing about it. It's narrow, and most of those who walk this path do so because of crisis.

But that's the beauty found on the narrow path of brokenness. It leads you to death so Jesus can bring you back to life as a *new* creation. Not a better version of the old you, but *new*! Brokenness starts closer to home than we might find comfortable. Hebrews 3:12 says, "Make sure that *your own hearts* are not evil and unbelieving, turning you away from the living God" (emphasis mine). As much as we might want to change our spouses—as much as we disapprove of their behavior and wish that they'd come to a place of brokenness—the path of brokenness begins with ourselves. The truth is, while the following verse says, "You must warn each other every day" (Hebrews 3:13), we can't control what other people will do. Yes, we can warn them, but ultimately, to take the narrow path of brokenness is first of all an individual decision. And when we are broken, there is a greater chance that God will use our brokenness as a witness to bring others to a place of brokenness in their own lives.

We must guard our hearts, because self-deception is the most dangerous type of deception. Self-deception will convince us that we are justified in our own behavior. Self-deception gives way to selfish choices rather than godly ones and often puts us back in the cycle of resentment. This passage in Hebrews goes on to say when we are deceived by sin, we become "hardened against God" (Hebrews 3:13). It doesn't say we *might* become hardened, but that we *will* become hardened against God.

The path of brokenness is hard, and the road is narrow, but brokenness brings us to a place where we can receive and give grace. This is where extraordinary thrives.

QUESTIONS

1. Is there anything that you need to confess to your spouse? Take some time to pray, asking God to examine your heart.

2. What are your natural coping mechanisms? How did these mechanisms develop? How might your spouse view these coping mechanisms?

3. What role does resentment play in your marriage? If any, how did that resentment come about?

4. What are the costs of choosing brokenness in your marriage? What are the benefits? Have you chosen brokenness? Why or why not?

9.

NO ORDINARY FORGIVENESS

IN OUR STORY, the affair gets all the attention, but what I (Trisha) have come to realize is that I had a forgiveness issue long before the affair. I had mastered the art of unforgiveness and felt clueless about what true forgiveness looked like.

Jesus knew we would struggle with this whole process of forgiveness. He knew forgiveness would have to be something we choose, not something we drift into. Look at this passage in Matthew:

> Peter came to [Jesus] and asked, "Lord, how often should I forgive someone who sins against me? Seven times?"
>
> "No, not seven times," Jesus replied, "but seventy times seven!"
>
> MATTHEW 18:21-22

Jesus tells Peter to forgive seventy times seven times, not because the person we forgive will need it that many times, but because resentment can have such a grip on our hearts that we need to forgive that often for our *own* healing. That is exactly what we realized as we walked through the cycle of forgiveness. Forgiveness is hard.

Christians aren't the first group of religious people to struggle with forgiveness. In the Gospel of John, a group of religious people catch a woman in the act of adultery. They have no intention of forgiving her. They have no compassion. They have no desire to dispense grace; they want condemnation. So they bring her out into the middle of the street and throw her at the feet of Jesus. With stones in their hands, they stand ready to bypass forgiveness and dispense justice. Here is how Jesus responds:

> When they kept on questioning him, he straightened up and said to them, "Let any one of you who is without sin be the first to throw a stone at her." Again he stooped down and wrote on the ground.
>
> At this, those who heard began to go away one at a time, the older ones first, until only Jesus was left, with the woman still standing there.
>
> JOHN 8:7-9, NIV

That is a great passage, but when I read it, it's easy for me to think, *What about her husband? He wasn't in that circle. He didn't do anything wrong. He had every right to throw stones.* What do you do with this idea of forgiveness when you have the right to dispense justice? What do you do when you have the right to throw stones?

The Christian thing to do is to follow Jesus' lead and put down your stone, but the truth is that the hurt is real. You've got this stone in your hand, and you know you're not supposed to throw it, but you can't let yourself drop it either.

One of the questions we always get—and it may be one of

the questions you had as you turned to this chapter—is, "How did Trisha ever forgive Justin? How in the world could she forgive him after what he did?" It is one of the most important questions you can ask, and one of the most amazing questions we have the honor of answering. After all, ordinary lives in resentment, but extraordinary lives in forgiveness.

JUSTIN:

I attended counseling alone every day. Two weeks after we separated, Trisha called me for the first time. When I saw her name on my cell phone, my stomach flip-flopped. It was the first time I had heard her voice in fifteen days. I had no idea what to expect; I was just thankful for her call.

She was gentle. She was soft spoken. She was open minded. If the Prodigal Son's father had had a cell phone, this was the kind of call he would have made. She asked a few questions. She made a few statements. We both cried. She didn't make any promises— just an offer to go to counseling with me.

Two days later, we began counseling together. I hoped to be home by the end of October. Our counselor hoped to have me home by Christmas. It would be a long journey. For the next thirty days, Trisha and I went to counseling together every day but Friday. We followed up our counseling appointments with long conversations on the phone. Long e-mail exchanges. Long talks over coffee or at Red Lobster.

More important than those conversations were the time and conversations I had with God. Sadly, it had been years since I had read the Bible for any purpose other than preparing a message. It had been years since I had spent time praying for anything other than church growth, church people, and church problems. God's presence had never been more tangible. God's voice had never been clearer. God's Word had never carried more power to illuminate the sin and darkness in my heart.

The things I was learning about myself were ugly. The affair wasn't the problem in our marriage; it was a visible and destructive symptom of an illness that had lived in my heart undetected. Insecurity and fear had ruled my life for years. They had given me an ability to manipulate people and situations in such a way that I would appear more put together and spiritual than I ever was. Years of woundedness, running, and hiding had finally caught up to me. I wanted to be different. I wanted to be healed. But I also wasn't sure I wanted to pay the price. It would take more courage and more faith than I'd ever had.

About a month after we began counseling, we came to a pivotal point in our recovery. Our counselor could see that trust was being rebuilt. Intimacy was being restored. What we did at this point would determine whether our marriage would experience health and recovery. This moment was huge. The counselor made it clear that if I had left anything out about the affair, any details at all, they had to be revealed. He told us to fast and pray for twenty-four hours and then come back—and I would share anything I had withheld.

We showed up together the next day. I spent the first ten minutes of our session sharing details about the affair that I had somehow withheld for the previous month. That was Trisha's breaking point. I had hurt her again. She left me there sitting in the counselor's office.

I called Tony and told him what I had done and asked if he could come pick me up. I went back to my room at his house and sobbed. I knew that my habitual inability to tell the truth had just delivered the knockout blow to my marriage. The past month had been a smoke screen to hide the disease that I couldn't break free from. About an hour after I arrived at the house, I received a phone call from a woman in our church. She told me that Trisha would file for divorce on Monday because I couldn't be a person of truth.

I was at my lowest low. My marriage was over.

Later that night, our counselor called me. He wanted to make sure I was okay. He had talked to Trisha, and she had told him that she was done with me. I felt hopeless. He said, "Maybe this is about your relationship with God more than your marriage."

He was right. For the past month, as much dependence as I'd felt on God, I'd really been focusing on what I needed to do to fix my marriage. What could I do to make up for the hurt? What could I say to take away the pain? How much could I change to finally be the husband Trisha deserved? What hoops did I need to jump through to have a better marriage?

The truth—though I didn't know it then—is that jumping through hoops will never give anyone an extraordinary marriage. Hoop jumping always leads to ordinary.

That night something clicked in my heart and mind. For the first time in my entire life, I desired my relationship with God more than anything else. Even if it meant I would be divorced, I knew I couldn't live the life I had been living for the past twelve years. I wanted to live in a right relationship with God, no matter my marital status.

I called a pastor friend of mine who had been my church-planting coach. He and I had met every Tuesday for the past three years for "accountability." I was supposed to share struggles and temptations and problems with him. I had failed him, too. I asked if I could come over that night to talk to him.

I arrived at Keith's house around eleven. I was terrified. I had never told anyone what I was going to share with him. I had convinced myself that if anyone knew about these things, I would lose everything. That fear had kept me silent with my board member by the creek, but that fear wasn't going to keep me silent tonight. The reality was that the effort to keep these things hidden had already cost me everything.

I sat at his dining room table, hands shaking, voice quivering, tears streaming down my face. I confessed to a ten-year addiction to pornography that I had never told anyone about. I told him I had been sexually abused as a kid and that I had never received help or shared it with anyone. I told him that all I wanted was to have a pure and authentic relationship with God. I was confident that Trisha was done with me, but I couldn't pretend with God anymore. I wanted a second chance with him now that everything else was gone.

Keith's response made me laugh. He said, "I'm going to pray for you, and I'm going to ask God to give you an opportunity to share this with Trisha." There was no way that would happen. Apart from the divorce courtroom, I would probably never again have the opportunity to speak to her. He prayed for me, hugged me, and tried to encourage me.

On Monday I came to the house to pick up the boys for school. Trisha appeared in the doorway and asked me to come in. I was content with getting the boys to school late, because being invited into the house trumped getting them to school on time. She sat down on the couch and said to me, "I have to know everything. Are you telling me everything?"

I said, "As far as that relationship goes, I've told you everything. But I have a lot more to tell you; I'm just not sure you want to know."

Trisha looked at me and said, "I want to know everything."

I asked the boys to wait upstairs and watch television until I came up to get them for school. It was just Trisha and I on the couch. I didn't want to hide anymore. I confessed to her what I had already confessed to Keith. I told her I was so ashamed that I had refused to admit to these things or get help. She was sobbing. I was heaving, I was crying so hard. "I haven't just been lying to you; I've been lying to myself, and I want to be a person of truth, even if you don't want to be married to me anymore."

In an act of grace and mercy unlike anything I'd ever seen or experienced, Trisha wiped my tears away and said, "Now we can begin again. Now we can start over."

We sat there in silence a few moments. I felt the Holy Spirit prompt me again. "I have one more thing to tell you," I said.

The look of defeat in her eyes felt so heavy. "What?" she said with suspicion.

"I was never recruited to play basketball at the University of Evansville," I admitted. "That's a lie I've been telling since I was eighteen. I've told it so many times, I've almost come to believe it myself."

To Trish, that may have seemed far less significant than the other things I confessed that morning, but for me, my redemption and the full redemption of our marriage hinged on that confession. I was not only committed to telling her the truth, I was finally committed to telling the truth to myself, no matter the cost.

That conversation wasn't the finish line—not even close. It was the starting point of a two-year journey through pain and loss and brokenness. That conversation gave birth to the grace, redemption, and restoration that continues to thrive in our marriage today. That conversation gave birth to the burden we now have to help couples put their ordinary marriages to death so that Christ can resurrect extraordinary marriages in their place.

TRISHA:

JOURNAL ENTRY—OCTOBER 17, 2005

Father, thank you for your amazing Word. Honestly, I have no idea what lies ahead. Please, please, please show me your will and the path I need to take. I pray you protect the hearts and minds of my church family. Lord, I pray for Justin. I miss him so much! I beg for wisdom and strength. Father, open doors for work. Please drop work in my lap, and give me the peace to know what the heck I'm supposed to do. I don't want to move a step without knowing it is your path, even if it is narrow! Please protect my boys' hearts. This is my prayer.

Over the first few days after Justin moved out, I began to strategize a plan for my life without Justin. This was what I feared most, but it was something I had to be prepared for. I opened new bank accounts; I had utilities put in my name; I dug into our budget and debt and got educated on the mess we were in financially. After several days of putting a plan together of what life would look like, it was now time to implement it. I was already working as a preschool teacher, but it wasn't enough to keep the lights on, so I took a front desk position at a vet clinic owned by a good friend of mine. I'll never forget answering my first call, perplexed that the lady on the other line not only wanted her dog "de-clawed" but that she kept calling it a "dewclaw." After five painful minutes of confusion, my friend explained to me the ABCs of pet anatomy.

Although I wasn't knocking it out of the park at the job and was still a bit shaky and clumsy in certain areas of my life, I felt solid in my relationship with God. I knew he was with me every step of the way, and one particular morning, I felt that God was prompting me to call Justin.

Voice shaking, I made the call, and to this day there are no words to describe what it was like to hear his voice after fifteen days of silence. That one call marked the beginning of being on the narrow path—no longer alone, but together.

We spent the next weeks in counseling, and even though it was painful and exhausting, we began growing closer together as we allowed the waterlines of our hearts to be lowered to a level we never had in the past. The problem was that I *still* had this heaviness in my heart and couldn't understand why.

Every session when Justin would share about the affair, I couldn't shake the feeling that he was still withholding truth. What I didn't realize was that as I pleaded with God to help me discern the difference between fear and truth, that feeling was the groaning of the Holy Spirit (which Paul talks about in Romans 8:26). On November 10, during the counseling session when Justin revealed the rest of the details about the affair, I understood why the groaning was so strong.

JOURNAL ENTRY—NOVEMBER 10, 2005

Shocking that I am back to square one! I hate you right now, God! . . . Why couldn't he have confessed all this when I asked? What's worse is that I know he's still not telling me the whole truth. Please reveal it to me through the power of your Holy Spirit, who will tell me the truth. I need to know, God. Please!

I'm certain I had this whole "confession" thing nailed down by the way I cried out to God that night. By morning, with some sleep to bring me back to my senses, I was painfully aware that confession is useless if it doesn't lead to transformation. So I prayed.

JOURNAL ENTRY—NOVEMBER 11, 2005

Father, I'm not sure what to say. I feel as if you have moved in my heart, yet I still feel really scared, hurt, and broken by what has taken place. I'm a messed-up sinner, I know, but you love me anyway. I want to love Justin like you love him, if that's even possible. Deep down, I love him beyond words, but his choices seem unbearable. What do I do with this sin? How do I move on? You are so amazing in your power that I know I can do anything with your strength in me. Help me to be strong and courageous. Help me to do everything in love.

Everything within me wanted to go numb and divorce Justin. It seemed impossible for him to speak the whole truth. He was the master manipulator, and I was done with that. But in this little prayer, I felt God whisper, *One more time.*

One more time for what? I thought. *If he was able to lie through these past couple of weeks, why would one more time make any difference?*

But that's why God is God and I'm not. This is life on the narrow path. Its curves are sharp, and you can't always see what's around the bend, so you have to constantly rely on the Father to know which way to turn. It's not a one-time deal where you hop on the path and it's easy going. It's a path that takes faith—faith that makes you stronger each time you choose to trust. It's a faith that allowed me to keep moving forward, knowing that I no longer had to carry the baggage because Jesus would carry it for me.

So that Monday morning, Justin walked into the house, and the only thing I could get to come out of my mouth was, "I want to know everything." And at those words, he told me everything. That feeling that had been with me all those years of our married life went away! We had finally hit rock bottom, and although it hurt when we landed, at least we had a surface to stand on. So together, with tears streaming from our faces, we stood on new ground.

Sometimes the difference between ordinary and extraordinary is simply our commitment to pursue the relationship at any cost.

JUSTIN & TRISHA:

THE CYCLE OF UNFORGIVENESS

Forgiveness is a word with a simple definition, yet the concept it represents is so hard to live out. There are some great quotes on forgiveness. There are Bible verses that talk about it. But when you read the word *forgiveness*, does a quote or Bible verse come to mind, or does it evoke an emotion or cause you to think of a certain person or situation? I (Trisha) think that for most of us, we associate forgiveness with a wound that has been inflicted on us.

Moving had become my wound. With each move, I experienced this intense sadness that at times felt like it could take my breath away. I was grieving. Moving meant leaving our church, home, and friends and starting all over again. I would take my grief and stuff it down deep into the back of my heart and mind. With each move, my grief turned to anger. Over time, my anger seemed to subside, but the reality is that my anger had become bitterness, a silent killer.

Maybe this is where you find yourself: your wound may be old or fresh, but your sadness is crippling, and the only way you know how to deal with it is to stay bitter.

Bitterness is like picking up a stone to throw and holding on to it so you'll have ammunition the next time you're wounded. We take our stones, hold them tight, and find comfort in them. But if we dwell in bitterness long enough, resentment is sure to follow. Over time I allowed my resentment to skew my view of Justin in other aspects of our relationship beyond just moving. My stone became ammunition in my fight to always be right, but the person I was hurting most was myself. Where resentment lives, intimacy dies.

This is what unforgiveness looks like: grief that is not mourned, which becomes anger that is not resolved, which turns into bitterness that is unconfessed, which becomes resentment that is unforgiven. But forgiveness calls us to lay down our stones and our rights in order to live in the extraordinary realm of true intimacy.

CONDITIONAL FORGIVENESS

The cycle of unforgiveness is understandable. We have been wounded. The people who wounded us were wrong. They owe us. Forgiving with conditions feels fair. We will forgive when they make up for what they've done.

But this expectation for compensation will always leave a void in your heart—there will be times when they *can't* make it up to you. Nothing they say will take away the pain. Nothing they do will ever erase the memory. Nothing they buy you will ever restore the hope that was lost.

Conditional forgiveness is not really forgiveness. Conditional forgiveness will do just as much damage as unforgiveness, even if it won't be as noticeable. Conditional forgiveness has the appearance of grace laced with the anticipation of performance. You will develop negative feelings if you expect compensation.

- You will become suspicious.
- You will become resentful.
- You will become insecure.
- You will manipulate and guilt-trip to get your way.
- You will live out of fear and worry.

The bar can never be set high enough for you to find the intimacy you are trying to re-create when you forgive only conditionally. When you are waiting for your spouse to make it up to you, your spouse will always fail, and you will be left searching for one more thing that will relieve the pain. The forgiveness you're looking for can only be found in Jesus. Trying to manufacture intimacy through your spouse's performance will never give you the marriage you desire. It will always leave you in ordinary.

EARNING YOUR FORGIVENESS

Before the affair, I (Justin) had a misguided view of forgiveness. I knew that God's forgiveness was unconditional, but I still thought I could earn more of his favor through my performance. I carried that view into my relationship with Trisha. She would be wounded by our move to a new city, and I thought I could make it up to her through my performance. I could make it up to her by providing her with stuff she wanted. I could make it up to her by trying really hard not to make her mad or hurt her again.

No one wants to be in a performance-based marriage. A performance-based marriage will never allow you to attain true forgiveness. It will leave you in a cycle of unforgiveness and ordinary. When you live with the mission of compensation in marriage:

- You work hard to not make your spouse mad.
- You walk on eggshells because you don't want to cause an argument.

- You stop being yourself because you feel shame and guilt.
- You feel that your spouse is more like your parent than your partner.

Do these traits sound similar to some of the other things we've talked about in this book? It's because they put you right back into the cycle. Living in a performance-based marriage will never build intimacy.

Here is the hard truth: you can't make up for whatever it is that you've done. You can't redeem yourself. When you spend your time and effort trying to perform and make up for your mistakes, you rob God of the work that he needs to do in your heart, and you put your spouse in the place of God. There is a better way—an *extraordinary* way. The redemption you desire can only be found in Jesus.

THE CYCLE OF FORGIVENESS

If there is a cycle of unforgiveness, then be assured there has to be a cycle of forgiveness. I (Trisha) had an unrelenting desire to figure it out, and as I did, I realized how the two can look eerily similar yet are polar opposites.

If you choose forgiveness, you will still feel grief. Grief is living in the truth that you have been wounded, and it needs to be dealt with rather than ignored. Often we Christians rob ourselves of the right to grieve, fearing that if we allow ourselves to feel the reality of our sadness, we somehow lack faith. But grief marks a pathway to begin the healing process.

When you forgive, you still experience anger. Grieving is essential to start the healing process, and anger is what propels you to take action. When people get angry, it causes them to take some kind of action, whether good or bad. What can become sin is the *action* we choose to take through our anger. But I believe that anger is a gift from God that allows us to step onto the path that grief has carved and to actively respond to that grief. Unforgiveness takes our anger and turns it into bitterness. But when we choose to forgive, our anger drives us to take the action God is calling us to: walking the path of brokenness we discussed in the last chapter.

But in this chasm of confusion, of figuring out what to do with our anger, many of us choose *blindness*. We believe that if we ignore our need to forgive, somehow our wound will heal on its own. We convince ourselves that when we get that promotion, or the new house, or the better house; when we get married; when we have children—that somehow these milestones and achievements will heal our wounds. So we forget our anger for a while, but when we realize that none of these things have provided the healing we thought they would, bitterness and resentment set in. Blindness just delays our inevitable bitterness.

Forgiveness is choosing to grieve and acknowledge that you have been wounded. Forgiveness uses anger to fuel your willingness to deal with your wound, and brokenness bridges the chasm between anger and healing. Brokenness is a complete surrender to God and his way, and with brokenness comes healing.

Here's what this looked like for me. My wound was not the affair but broken trust. With each move, I felt that Justin had broken my trust. Now with the affair, I had to grieve the loss of my marriage, my best friend, and my church family. I became angry and begged God to show me the path to healing. In God's amazing grace, what he asked was that I become broken before him and recognize my own need for his grace and forgiveness. When I lived with a posture of gratitude for Jesus and his work on the cross, it prepared my heart to forgive and experience healing.

This is what forgiveness looks like: grief that is mourned, which turns into anger, which causes you to choose brokenness instead of bitterness, which allows you to experience healing.

THE DIFFERENCE BETWEEN FORGIVENESS & TRUST

A common mistake some people make is to confuse forgiveness with trust. Forgiveness, according to Scripture, should be offered unconditionally. In fact, if there are conditions, it isn't forgiveness. But trust has to be earned.

The currency of any relationship is trust. I (Justin) had not just broken Trisha's trust with the adulterous relationship; I had broken her trust in a lot of different ways. My decisions to move us frequently broke her trust. The way I creatively worked our finances broke trust. My exaggerating and withholding truth broke trust. The pornography addiction I admitted to revealed a ten-year period of being untrustworthy. A few months after the affair, Trisha and I were talking about forgiveness. With tears in her eyes she said, "I know I can forgive you; I just don't know if I can ever trust you."

So many marriages drift to ordinary and stay there because they have confused these two aspects of a relationship: forgiveness and trust. When we've been hurt or betrayed or abused or lied to, trust is broken in that relationship. When trust is broken, so is intimacy. Being fully known isn't possible when there is a lack of trust.

There is no doubt that forgiveness is a process, but trust is a prized possession. Once your trust has been broken, it becomes even more valuable, and it becomes imperative to know the difference between forgiveness and trust. If you are struggling to figure out the balance between these two important aspects to your relationship, can I give you this advice? Offer forgiveness freely; offer trust slowly.

Healing doesn't come all at once. When you've been hurt, lied to, or betrayed, your heart is in a vulnerable state. What you want most is what you used to have: before the porn, before the sexting, before the lie, before the cheating, before the Facebook relationship. The temptation is to equate forgiveness with trust. When you do that, you short-circuit your own healing and the restoration of the one who has broken your trust.

Trust is built one day at a time, one act at a time. And it is built *s-l-o-w-l-y.* When Trisha and I were separated, she asked me to bring the kids home by 7:00 p.m. so she could get them ready for bed. I always had them there before 7:00. I got to see them three to four evenings per week, and there was not one time I brought them back later than she asked. I didn't realize it at the time, but that was a big deal to her. Before the affair, I rarely came home when I said I would. I was rarely on time going *anywhere*, so for me to be on time in getting the kids home made a huge impression on her. I was beginning to regain her trust.

Jesus communicates this idea in a powerful way in the story of the woman caught in adultery mentioned at the beginning of this chapter. He said to her, "Neither do I [condemn you]. Go and sin no more" (John 8:11). In this statement Jesus offered forgiveness ("Neither do I [condemn you]") but also gave the woman an opportunity to earn trust ("Go and sin no more").

Give the person who has hurt you an opportunity to earn your trust. Don't withhold forgiveness in this process. Communicate honestly and openly, and allow the Holy Spirit to prompt you. You shouldn't be fearful or paranoid, rather wise and discerning.

If you have broken trust in a relationship, it can be so easy for you to confuse forgiveness with trust. I know the feeling: *If you had really forgiven me, we wouldn't be having these conversations.* Ask yourself this question: *Has my spouse not forgiven me, or does my spouse not trust me?*

Your marriage may not have the trust issues ours did. But anytime you wound your spouse, trust is broken. In small and sometimes unnoticeable ways, but broken nonetheless. You can do your part in the healing process by earning trust after forgiveness has been extended.

My guess is that it will be much easier for your spouse to forgive you than to trust you. Pay the price. Seek to do the little things that will earn trust.

In every relationship, forgiveness should be free, but trust must be earned.

CONTINUAL FORGIVENESS: AN ILLUSTRATION

I (Trisha) convinced myself about a year into our restoration process that I had mastered forgiveness. I felt like God was prompting me to write my best friend a letter. I told her I forgave her. I told her that in my brokenness, God had helped me recognize that she was broken too. I told her that I understood the part Justin played in it all. I told her I missed her and her family. It was one of the hardest things I have ever done, but I felt like it brought closure and a sense of pride that I had been obedient to God. I had truly mastered forgiveness.

A month went by, then six months, and finally a year passed, and I heard nothing in response to my letter. *Nothing.* I was devastated and hurt all over again. The healing I thought I would find through forgiveness only brought me more pain. In my pain I looked for my stone and stayed armed in my anger toward her.

I sat down to journal because that's the "Christian thing" to do. I tried to read about forgiveness to stop the steam from billowing out my ears. Not only was I angry toward my friend, but I was also angry with God! I remember telling God, *You have no idea what is like to be betrayed by a good friend! You have no idea what it's like to suffer the consequences of other people's choices when you did nothing wrong! You have no idea what it's like to offer something and have it rejected.*

As I looked for Bible verses to calm me down, I found the famous seventy-times-seven passage and continued reading the story of the unmerciful servant:

> The Kingdom of Heaven can be compared to a king who decided to bring his accounts up to date with servants who had borrowed money from him. In the process, one of his debtors was brought in who owed him millions of dollars. He couldn't pay, so his master ordered that he be sold—along with his wife, his children, and everything he owned—to pay the debt.

But the man fell down before his master and begged him, "Please, be patient with me, and I will pay it all." Then his master was filled with pity for him, and he released him and forgave his debt.

But when the man left the king, he went to a fellow servant who owed him a few thousand dollars. He grabbed him by the throat and demanded instant payment.

His fellow servant fell down before him and begged for a little more time. "Be patient with me, and I will pay it," he pleaded. But his creditor wouldn't wait. He had the man arrested and put in prison until the debt could be paid in full.

When some of the other servants saw this, they were very upset. They went to the king and told him everything that had happened. Then the king called in the man he had forgiven and said, "You evil servant! I forgave you that tremendous debt because you pleaded with me. Shouldn't you have mercy on your fellow servant, just as I had mercy on you?"

MATTHEW 18:23-33

For most of us, we read this passage and immediately realize who the bad guy is. *I* read this passage and knew that I was the king because I *did* forgive! But as I read and reread this story, it dawned on me that the king forgave with no conditions. The king was left with a debt that still had to be repaid even if his servant couldn't pay. It was in that moment that I realized I was the unmerciful servant. I sat there feeling the sting of not receiving a response from the letter, but now I had to put my stone down *again* to listen to what God was teaching me in my understanding of forgiveness. I heard God whisper two words: *I do.*

I do know what it's like to be betrayed by a close friend.

I do know what it's like to suffer the consequences when I did nothing wrong.

I do know what it's like to offer all of me only to be rejected.

I do know your pain.

I was not the king but the unmerciful servant. Jesus Christ is the king. Jesus took on the debt of my sin when he died on the cross, regardless of whether I would believe in him. He knows what it means to have to forgive—he is the expert.

Forgiveness is only true forgiveness when you forgive regardless of the person's response. Grace is unmerited favor, a gift offered with no strings attached. Forgiveness is a gift that flows from grace. In forgiveness, we give up our right to throw our stones in retaliation for the hurt the other has caused us.

Christ loved us enough that he laid down his life so we could have life forever with him. He owed us nothing yet gave up everything. His call for us to forgive is about more than the person who wounded us. Rather, through brokenness, we say, "God, I lay it all before you. I give you my pain, my bitterness, my heavy stones."

And with that surrender comes the kind of healing that only Jesus can give. With healing comes *freedom*—freedom to live a life without stones. Freedom to live in the extraordinary with the Father, who is always trustworthy. Freedom in the love of a Savior who is the same yesterday, today, and forever.

Spouses in extraordinary marriages live in the awareness of the grace and forgiveness given them by the Father. They embrace grief, anger, brokenness, and forgiveness rather than ignore them. They live in the knowledge that forgiveness is a process, not a one-time choice, and that it may take seventy times seven to finally feel reconciled. And they live in the grace to keep that forgiveness flowing.

Maybe you have fought your whole marriage to be right. You don't think your husband respects you. You don't feel like your wife believes in you. So this resentment you hold on to is your way of proving yourself or of having the upper hand. This anger you keep just under the surface of your heart is a part of you. You wouldn't know who you were without it. Your anger allows you to be in control. Living in the hurt of the past allows you to brace yourself to deal with the disappointments and hurt in the future. You find your identity in your resentment.

If that's the case, the truth is that there is a part of your heart you are not just withholding from the person you can't forgive. You are withholding that part of your heart from God. And God longs to heal you, to free you, to form you and shape you into the person you were created to be.

Maybe this resentment you've learned to accept has nothing to do with your spouse. You take it out on your spouse, but it isn't really about him or her. Your past hurts have made a home in your marriage and in the process have made your marriage ordinary. You were abused. You were overlooked. You were raped. You were taken advantage of. She broke up with you. He lied to you. She never said she was sorry. Your dad never came back. Your mom never told you she loved you. Your friend abandoned you when you needed him the most.

In reality, you are terrified that if you forgive, you will be admitting defeat. If you forgive, they win. But forgiveness doesn't excuse their behavior. Forgiveness prevents their behavior from destroying your heart. Forgiveness prevents forfeiting your future by not living in your past. Forgiveness prepares you to move from ordinary to extraordinary.

When you forgive, the person who hurt you doesn't win—*Christ* wins. He wins another part of your heart. When you forgive, you allow Christ to have not only more of your heart but more of your marriage. Where forgiveness lives, intimacy can be restored.

Author Anne Lamott says in her book *Traveling Mercies*, "Not forgiving is like drinking rat poison and then waiting for the rat to die." Who do you need to forgive? Forgiveness leads to healing, healing leads to intimacy, and intimacy leads to extraordinary.

QUESTIONS

1. What wounds in your life have a tendency to keep you in the cycle of unforgiveness? Why?

2. Think about the difference between forgiveness and trust. Have you confused the two in your relationships? How can you maintain the distinction between them?

3. Is there someone in your life you have forgiven conditionally? Why have you attached conditions to your forgiveness?

4. In the cycle of forgiveness it's hard to recognize when and how to move on. Where do you find yourself in the cycle?

10.

NO ORDINARY HEALING

WHAT IF THE WOUNDS could be forgiven but not healed? What if our marriage wouldn't survive? What if we had done our best to put the pieces back together, but our best just wasn't enough? Those were the questions that dominated our hearts as we attempted to rebuild our marriage, our family, and our lives. As Trisha and I (Justin) pursued healing for our marriage, we also pursued healing individually. It was our individual healing that made the process complicated.

We both needed healing, but for very different reasons. I was trying to recover from how much I had hurt Trisha and was daily coming to terms with the number of people I had wounded. At the same time, I had to figure out how I had allowed my heart to get so dark and what was the root cause of my choices. It was over-whelming at times. Trisha was overwhelmed with her own pain, loss, and grief, yet was daily choosing to fight through her wounds to love me—sometimes because she wanted to and sometimes just out of obedience to God.

The reality was that an apology wouldn't make everything okay. A two-month separation and hours of counseling wouldn't solve our problems. Making promises to be better or to do better wouldn't help. Utter and complete destruction of the person I was and the marriage we had would be necessary. God wasn't interested in making me a better person. Complete healing—the kind of healing God desires—would only come through allowing the old me and our old marriage to die.

In his book *The Cost of Discipleship*, Dietrich Bonhoeffer wrote, "When Christ calls a man, he bids him come and die." For the first time in my life and in our marriage, the greatest desire of my heart was to be healed and whole, not "fixed" and fake. I realized that God is the God of resurrections. But in order for something to be brought back to life, it has to die. Living things aren't brought back to life; dead things are. Was I willing to allow the parts of my heart that had led me to an ordinary marriage to die? If I was willing, what did that even look like?

JUSTIN:

From the moment all the truth was revealed until I moved back with Trisha, we were separated for two and a half months. Our counselor suggested for the sake of our marriage and for the sake of the church that we should move away from Noblesville. It would be easier for us to begin again and easier for the church to heal if I wasn't visible or available. So in February 2006, we moved for the eleventh time in our ten and a half years of marriage. Trisha had promised to forgive me, but it was a daily battle for her.

While Trisha is the most important relationship in my life, she wasn't the only person I had damaged. I prayed that God would give me an opportunity to apologize to everyone I had hurt, and a few weeks after I moved back with Trisha, I got a phone call from Dave Rodriguez, the pastor at Grace Community Church. He wanted to meet with me.

Upon my resignation from Genesis, Dave and Keith and some others from Grace led our elders and staff through the process of informing our congregation about what had happened and walked them through the steps they would need to take to protect the church and allow the church to heal. So Dave was not only close to our church, he was directly impacted by my sinful choices. I had no idea what to expect at our meeting. To say I was nervous is an understatement.

I arrived at Starbucks, and Dave was inside waiting for me. He stood up and gave me a hug and tears filled his eyes. We sat down, and I recounted for him the long, dark journey I had made to cheat on God, my wife, the church, Dave, his staff, every person who had supported us, and so many others. I also told him of the restoration God had begun in my heart and the way God was bringing healing to Trisha and me and our family through counseling. He was genuinely happy for us and proud of the steps I had taken.

At the end of our time together, he said something that changed me, my marriage, and everything I do and say to this day. He said, "I want you to know I am praying a Lamentations 3 prayer for you. Specifically, I am praying Lamentations 3:16 over you."

I had no idea what Lamentations 3 was about, nor did I know what verse 16 of Lamentations 3 said. I said, "I really appreciate that. . . . Do you mind telling me what Lamentations 3:16 says?"

"It says that God will grab you by the back of the head and crush your teeth on gravel. That is my prayer for you."

Huh? Maybe Dave meant he was praying *John* 3:16 prayers for me. I like John 3:16. But he said, "If you are going to find true healing from this, God is going to have to destroy you first. Lamentations 3 is my prayer for you." We hugged, and I left.

When I got home that afternoon, I immediately grabbed my Bible and went to Lamentations 3:16-18 (NIV):

> He has broken my teeth with gravel;
> he has trampled me in the dust.

I have been deprived of peace;
> I have forgotten what prosperity is.
So I say, "My splendor is gone
> and all that I had hoped from the LORD."

I wanted true healing, but what did it look like to have my teeth broken with gravel? I had been a Christian for over twenty years and had been a pastor for ten, yet I had no idea what having your teeth smashed by gravel was about. But I began to pray Lamentations 3:16 for me too. I asked God to break my teeth with gravel. I asked him to trample me in the dust and to break my bones. It felt weird at first to ask God to break me, to smash me, to trample me rather than just praying that he fix our marriage. When Trisha and I had had problems in the past, I'd pray a quick prayer, but most of my effort was spent trying to fix what she was upset about, reading a marriage book, or just attempting to do better.

The first step in having my teeth broken with gravel was finding a new job. The only thing I had ever been was a pastor. When I left the church, I had no idea what I was going to do with the rest of my life. I had forfeited my right to be a pastor, but I had no other job experience as an adult. I had no clue what to do. Feeling like part of my healing was simply doing the right thing, I needed a job to provide for our basic needs until I could figure out my next career. So I went to P. F. Chang's to apply for a job. I was a huge P. F. Chang's fan and felt that if I was going to wait tables, at least I'd love the food I'd bring home at the end of the night. I was hired and started the next day.

I went from speaking to over five hundred people each weekend to, "Would you like white or brown rice?" It was humbling and humiliating.

It was exactly what I needed.

One night as I was closing my section, I had a table of several high school students who had come for dinner after their school dance. They were loud and rude, made a huge mess, and hung out so long that I was one of the last servers to leave. After they left, I was on my hands and knees under their table, sweeping up rice and crushed-up fortune cookies with my hands into a dustpan. I stood up and looked on the table. They had left me a measly five-dollar tip!

I thought, *I am busting my butt cleaning up after these kids who couldn't care less about me. When was the last time I did this at home? When was the last time I gave to Trisha what I'm giving to P. F. Chang's for a flimsy tip?* Lamentations 3 was starting to make sense.

I worked at P. F. Chang's for a little over two months. God taught me more in that time about himself, his presence, and the power he has to provide than I learned in five years at Bible college.

Our marriage had been ordinary for so many years because I had allowed God to "improve" me, not re-create me. I had tried to escape the crushing of teeth and the breaking of bones and in the process had also forgone the faithfulness and mercies and salvation and compassion of God. I had created the best life and marriage I knew how to create, but my best was simply ordinary. God wanted to give us something more, but the "more" he had in mind I couldn't produce. It would have to come from him.

TRISHA:

Moving twenty minutes away from the city where we planted the church gave brokenness a whole new meaning. We were moving to a city where we had no friends and this time no church welcoming us. We had no identity other than being a family moving from everything and everybody we loved. We moved with help from Justin's dad and our friend and real estate agent Chris. Honestly, despite our many moves being a touchy subject for me, I was completely content with this new chapter of our lives as long as I didn't have to make new friends. Although I was willing to work on our marriage, I was done with friendship.

But—seriously—about an hour after arriving at our new house, not just one, but *two* of our neighbors came over to welcome us.

One of our neighbors shared with us the names of all the families on our street including a pastor who led a nearby church. It took everything I had not to roll my eyes, give a three-snap "talk to the hand," and tell him, "Let me define the relationship here: I'm not up for making friends, so could you please not come to my house ever again? Thanks!"

But I didn't. I shyly extended my hand and introduced myself and our boys to his boys, who were, of course, the exact same ages. I had been obedient in moving because I knew it was the right thing to do, but I became so focused on the move itself that I hadn't thought through how the story would unfold once we got there.

In the back of my mind I had hoped that moving would allow our family to move on. No longer would we have to fear running into people from church or my best friend. No longer would we have intense counseling sessions and conversations about "what's next" for our family. "What's next" was here, and I was ready to move on. It was obvious by my first encounter with my neighbors that parts of me were still very raw. The path of brokenness meant that *I* needed to pray a Lamentations 3 prayer too—a prayer not just for the present but also for wounds inflicted in the past.

Despite my initial coldness, God used this amazing block of people to help me begin a journey I thought I would never be ready or willing to embrace. God was still writing my story, just not quite the way I would have written it.

When Justin and I started our restoration journey, we realized that in order to find extraordinary healing, we had to turn back the pages of our story to well before the chapters of our marriage, our ministry, and the affair were written. We had to go back to the beginning of our hurt and pain in order to understand how they had shaped us into who we had become.

As scary as it was to examine our pasts, I desperately wanted to find and examine whatever unresolved brokenness I was carrying. As I began to investigate my past, what I thought was *my* story alone was actually interwoven with other stories found in my parents, sister, brother, and the other people who came in and out of my life. And by doing this, I discovered a lot about who I was—and I didn't like the impostor I found.

JUSTIN:

I discovered that to have a different marriage, I had to be a different person. That wasn't going to happen without confronting the darkest parts of my heart. From the outside, the issues we faced seemed obvious: my pornography addiction and my choice to have an affair. But deep down I knew those things were symptoms of a much bigger disease. If I could diagnose that illness, then true healing would happen.

Brennan Manning's *The Ragamuffin Gospel* had been one of my favorite books for years. I read it shortly after I got out of college, and it revolutionized my view of grace. As I sat in our home office late one night and looked over at our bookshelf, I noticed another Brennan Manning book that we owned but had never read. It was called *Abba's Child*. Trisha and I had been reading together each night—well, *I* would read aloud while she "rested her eyes"—and I thought this would be a good book for us. I had no idea at the time that God would use *Abba's Child* to break my teeth against gravel and restore my soul all at the same time.

In *Abba's Child*, there is a chapter called "The Impostor." Manning describes "the impostor" as the false self we create to preserve our image and keep ourselves free from the displeasure of others. As Manning described the impostor, I realized the impostor's direct assault on intimacy. The impostor's goal is not to be fully known; it is to be known only to the degree that it helps maintain our image, our reputation, or our lifestyle. Here are the characteristics that Manning gives of the impostor:

- The impostor lives in fear.
- The impostor is preoccupied with acceptance and approval.

- The impostor is what he does.
- The impostor inspires us to attach value to things that have no value.
- The impostor is a liar.
- The impostor demands to be noticed.

How much of my life had I spent living in fear? Fear of failure, fear of others' opinions, and fear of letting others down dominated my life and ministry. I desired the acceptance and approval of others more than I desired the acceptance and approval of God. I found my identity in my role as a pastor. I had confused my calling with my identity. No longer was my calling an overflow of my identity in Christ; rather, my relationship with Christ was an add-on to my role as a pastor. I was a liar. I had not only mastered lying to others, I was an expert at lying to myself. I did all of this in an effort to be noticed.

Manning cut straight to my heart with another statement:

> While the impostor draws his identity from past achievements and the adulation of others, the true self claims identity in its belovedness. We encounter God in the ordinariness of life: not in the search for spiritual highs and extraordinary, mystical experiences but in our simple presence in life.

I had learned to find my value and significance in how successful I was and in what other people thought or believed about me. I never learned to find my value and significance as a child of God. God was answering my Lamentations 3 prayers as I took on my impostor.

The wounds I created and perpetuated by allowing the impostor to exist had prevented me from experiencing the full capacity of God's love. When we do not live in the fullness of God's love, we are incapable of loving others fully. I could have read every marriage book, listened to every great sermon about marriage, and gone to a marriage conference every weekend, but until I dealt with the false self I had created, I wouldn't experience healing. And without healing, I would be left with only a partial intimacy.

TRISHA:

Christmas morning 2006 could go down as one of the best Christmases ever. We had lived in our new house for almost a year, and that morning it finally felt like home. The boys had finished a full semester in their new schools and had made tons of new friends. Justin was killing it at his new job as an executive recruiter and even won rookie of the year. There was a sense of joy in our home not just for the awesome gifts we shared with each other, but for the best gift of all: our family! Our family was together, and it seemed that even our three-year-old understood the significance of that.

As exhilarating as it was to celebrate that we had survived a whole year together, Justin and I both struggled to believe that God would do a "new thing" in us. There were still more questions than answers for how this new life would unfold. With each passing day, Justin and I felt excitement over how we were seeing each other in ways we never had before. Our love for each other *was* different. Our relationship had become honest, passionate, fun, and exciting. I can't help but smile as I type those words, knowing they are still true for who we are today. But as awesome as our relationship was becoming, there was a fear to match it. We had become so in love with each other that both of us were terrified that we would mess it up.

What if we really aren't becoming "new creations"?
What if Justin struggles again?
What if I wake up one day and decide this is too hard to get over?
What if . . . ?

"What if" was starting to attack our hearts and minds. Although we authentically loved being together, we realized our motives were often fear of the "what if" rather than living in the "what is." Neither of us hung out with friends. I met Justin three to four times a week for lunch. We called each other multiple times a day just to check in. We made sure we went to bed together every night. We were trying really hard to do things differently.

Each night we read together (okay, Justin read aloud, and I would listen to half a chapter before falling asleep), looking for someone to teach us how to work harder. We had already read a few books, but one night we started a book that not only validated that God was making us new but also explained the how and why behind it all. That night there was no falling asleep. I listened wide eyed, with ears open to what Justin was reading. *Abba's Child*, by Brennan Manning gave no formula, no prescription, but rather the simple truth laced with perplexing human brokenness and a call to live as Abba's child. His words of wisdom that true healing doesn't come from working harder but from surrender breathed freedom into a fearful couple.

As Justin fought to conquer the impostor within, I struggled to surrender my distrust. As I've shared before, I love people. I love seeing people victorious, redeemed, and restored. But it wasn't till I read these words from *Abba's Child* that I realized the root issue for my lack of trust:

> My identity as Abba's child is not an abstraction or a tap dance into religiosity. It is the core truth of my existence. Living in the wisdom of accepted tenderness profoundly affects my perception of reality, the way I respond to people and their life situations.

Manning goes on to say this:

> The betrayals and infidelities in my life are too numerous to count. I still cling to the illusion that I must be morally impeccable, other people must be sinless, and the one I

love must be without human weakness. But whenever I allow anything but tenderness and compassion to dictate my response to life—be it self-righteous anger, moralizing, defensiveness, the pressing need to change others, carping criticism, frustration at others' blindness, a sense of spiritual superiority, a gnawing hunger of vindication—I am alienated from my true self. My identity as Abba's child becomes ambiguous, tentative, and confused.

I struggled with trusting that God was making me a new creation. I couldn't fully surrender to the thought that "the old life is gone; a new life has begun" (2 Corinthians 5:17) because it never seemed to prove true. In the past when I *would* authentically and deeply love people with compassion and tenderness, I often didn't get the same in return. While I love seeing people succeed, it crushed me when they would break my trust in the process. The affair was my worst nightmare, not only for the obvious reasons but because it went against the core of who I am. *Faithfulness breeds faithfulness,* I thought. *If I am faithful to you, then you should be faithful to me.*

In theory, this is reasonable, but what I was really saying—or demanding, rather—is that other people must be sinless, and the one I love must be without human weakness. No one, other than Jesus, can live up to this standard. We were all born sinners, and although we can live righteously through the power of Christ, we will never live perfect and blameless lives. God's mercies are new every morning because he knew we would need them every day. I had to embrace the painful reality that my view of myself masked a dangerous illusion that I would never be unfaithful, when in truth I am unfaithful to God every day. Yet in his great love and his daily mercies, he still chooses to love me. The question that remained was, would I surrender to this new life that would ask me to do the same?

My new life in him is daily choosing to surrender my need to find my identity in the way people respond to the way I love them, forgive them, and trust them. This is the impostor that tells me to stop trusting others because they will let me down. I have lived most of my life with this impostor, and it's a struggle I still face today. It's a struggle I have to surrender and confess to Justin and those close to me when my impostor threatens to take over, shut me down, and keep me prisoner in the muck and mire of bitterness and self-protective anger.

Needless to say, Justin and I had no idea how much an impact *Abba's Child* would have on who we are today. The book you hold in your hands was created in part from the almost decade-long research project of two people who together have been trying to live in surrender as Abba's children. I am so thankful that the extraordinary is possible through a life surrendered to God.

JUSTIN & TRISHA:

FORGIVING YOURSELF

One of the takeaway points that Trisha and I (Justin) got from Brennan Manning's *Abba's Child* is that we are to find the whole of our identity in who we are in relation to God, and God sees us as his dearly loved children—children he loved enough to sacrifice his Son for in order to obtain their forgiveness. But we don't always live in this identity, especially after we fail on a large scale.

For about a year after the affair, I lived in shame and guilt and remorse. There wasn't a day when I didn't think about all the damage I'd caused; all the hurt I'd inflicted; all the relationships I'd destroyed. I knew that Trisha had forgiven me, but my heart couldn't accept it.

Our marriage in many ways was in recovery mode, and we were growing in our love for one another. But the daily pain of my decisions ate away at my heart. It affected my view of myself. It affected my relationship with my kids. It affected my relationship with God.

I felt undeserving. I felt unworthy. I felt like I should be unloved.

I remember standing in the kitchen one evening and breaking down in tears. I knew God and Trisha had forgiven me, but I couldn't forgive myself. Trisha said to me, "Grace is only grace if you accept it. I've worked so hard to extend it to you, and you aren't accepting it. I forgive you. I think it's time you forgive yourself."

Those words were like water to my parched soul. I didn't think I could ever forgive myself.

If I forgive myself, doesn't that mean I'm getting away with something?

If I forgive myself, doesn't that make it seem like I'm not paying for what I've done?

If I forgive myself, who will remind me of how much of a screwup I am?

But these thoughts did not allow me to see myself as Abba's child. In God's eyes I was already forgiven. To live as if this weren't true prevented me from finding all of my identity in my relationship with God.

Second Corinthians 7:10 says something so powerful: "Godly sorrow brings repentance that leads to salvation and leaves no regret, but worldly sorrow brings death" (NIV). In other words, true repentance paves the way for us to forgive ourselves. When we are more brokenhearted over the *act* of our sin than the *consequences* of our sin, that is godly sorrow. Worldly sorrow is being sorry for getting caught or being sorry for the consequences of our sin more than for the sin itself. That type of sorrow will leave regret in your heart, and it doesn't lead to life.

Shame and regret can leave you in an ordinary marriage just as much as the resentment and unforgiveness we've talked about in other chapters. If one person in a relationship has forgiven but the other consistently lives as a second-class citizen, not feeling worthy to be a part of the other's life, there is no soil for grace to take root.

Maybe the best thing we can do for our spouses is give them permission to forgive themselves.

Your marriage may feel ordinary, and the intimacy you desire may not feel attainable. You may be the only person who can set your spouse free to forgive him- or herself. If you are the person who messed up and you consistently live in shame and guilt and you've been offered forgiveness, receive it.

Shame isn't attractive. Guilt isn't a good basis from which to build intimacy. To quote my beautiful wife, "You've been forgiven. I think it's about time to forgive yourself."

BETTER OR BRAND NEW?

We have a tendency to equate healing with being fixed. If we can fix ourselves, if we can fix our spouses, if we can fix our marriages, then everything will be better. Can I (Justin) share something with you? God doesn't want to fix your marriage; he wants to heal your heart. The truth is that both you and your spouse bring a past into your marriage. You bring sins and hurts and disappointments. Maybe you were raped in high school. Maybe you had a one-night stand in college. Maybe you were physically or sexually abused as a kid. Maybe you had an abortion. Maybe you cheated on your first wife and are now married to the woman with whom you cheated.

What Trisha and I have come to understand in our marriage is that the depth of restoration and intimacy we experience today is in direct proportion to our willingness to understand our hurts and completely surrender them to the redeeming power of Christ. God promises to re-create you—that is how committed to your healing he is. God doesn't want you to be *better*, he wants you to be *brand new*.

What hinders the healing of our hearts and pushes us to pursue being "fixed" is our tendency toward self-preservation. Our own reputations so often take precedence over the wholeness and healing that God longs to give us. For us to develop extraordinary marriages, we have to get to the core of our ordinary lives.

There are so many couples who wear themselves out merely trying to fix their marriages when God longs to heal their hearts.

Maybe that is where you are as you read this book. You are tired. You are exhausted. You have tried everything you know to be a better husband, but it isn't enough. Maybe you have tried everything you can to make your husband happy, but it isn't enough. Things get better for a week or a month or a year, but you come back to this place of discouragement or discontentment.

When Trisha and I experienced problems or issues in our marriage, I had always asked the question "what?" I thought, *Just tell me what to do. Just give me the steps to take to be a better husband, to be a better father, to be a better Christian.*

Maybe that is where you are as it relates to this chapter. Maybe that is where you are as it relates to this book. *Just give me the steps to have a better marriage. Just tell me what to do.*

I think one of the great tragedies in the church today is that we've too often reduced our relationship with God to a checklist of what we can do to improve, rather than focusing on who we can become as Christ transforms us. "What" might change your behavior, a little at a time. But asking "what" brings something inferior for which we've settled for far too long: incremental change.

INCREMENTAL CHANGE *Is this the right word?*

Incremental change is you and your spouse doing your best and working your hardest to stay married or to not get divorced. Incremental change makes big promises but lasts only a short time. Incremental change is change you are in control of. Incremental change is you working harder to stop the things you keep messing up. Incremental change, at its core, has you at the center trying to be better today than you were yesterday. Incremental change tells you if you try hard enough, you can cuss less, drink less, click on pornography less, eat less, lose your temper less, spend less, lust less, lie less, cheat less. Incremental change is motivated by guilt and shame and feelings of incompetence and failure. Incremental change convinces you that if you can endure the pain of trying harder to cover up your sin and get better, then no one needs to know; you can overcome this. Incremental change doesn't allow you to experience grace and forgiveness because you are constantly trying to make up for the sin in your life. Incremental change carries a small price tag up front, but it robs you for the rest of your life of the peace and joy and victory God longs to provide.

TRANSFORMATIONAL CHANGE

There is another option. God offers transformational change. Transformational change is about surrender, vulnerability, and transparency; humility and dependency. Transformational change at its core aims to destroy you, and if you are willing to pay that price, it will totally destroy every part of you. Transformational change is messy and bloody and it hurts deep and it will cost you everything. It is pulling all of your junk out and laying it on the table for all to see no matter what they think about you. Transformational change is committed not just to dealing with the symptoms of your issues but to peeling back layer after painful layer of your past, your dysfunction, and your sin until the core problem is exposed. Transformational change is recognizing that on even your best day, you are a failure and a sinner and your only hope is grace. Transformational change is knowing you can never try hard enough to overcome your desire to drink, cuss, lust, gorge, lie, and cheat. What you *can* do is surrender to the God of resurrection power, allowing him not only to destroy you, but also to bring you back to life. In order to be brought back to life, one has to die.

The problem with transformation is that it usually starts with affliction. Jeremiah says in Lamentations 3:1, "I am the one who has seen the afflictions that come from the rod of the LORD's anger." When the Babylonians destroyed Jerusalem and exiled its people to a distant country, they left Jeremiah behind. Jeremiah is known as the "weeping prophet" for good reason: he saw the destruction of his city, and he mourned what he saw. This is the context of the book of Lamentations, a five-chapter song of sadness over what had happened to Jeremiah's beloved city. But despite the horrible events that Jeremiah witnessed, he was still able to say, "The faithful love of the LORD never ends! His mercies never cease. Great is his faithfulness; his mercies begin afresh each morning" (Lamentations 3:22-23).

And, indeed, it took the destruction of Jerusalem and the exile of its people to bring them to a place of brokenness. Once they had been in exile for around seventy years, the Lord set in motion a plan to bring them home. Without the brokenness resulting from the pain of exile, the people wouldn't have experienced the repentance necessary for the joy of return.

Author C. S. Lewis said, "God whispers to us in our pleasures, speaks in our conscience, but shouts in our pain: it is His megaphone to rouse a deaf world." Often God's path to healing and transformation involves pain. The reason we experience little transformation is because we have equated numbness with contentment. But living a numb life and living in a numb marriage only prevent us from becoming the people and the spouses God longs for us to be.

Humans have created incremental change because we don't like the pain of transformational change. Maybe the difference between ordinary and extraordinary is found in the difference between incremental change and transformational change. Healing—*extraordinary* healing—is found in transformational change.

You don't need incremental change in your marriage; you need transformational change. You don't need an improved version of the old you; you need a brand-new you. You don't need a slight improvement in your marriage; you need a complete transformation. The great news is that God offers to transform you. God offers to give you a new life. God longs to give you an extraordinary marriage.

The bad news is that it will come at a price—a very high price: your complete selves. But your life on the other side of confession and repentance and pain and surrender and forgiveness will be the life you've been pretending to have all of the years you've tried to change a little at a time.

Surrender will bring about healing, and healing will allow you to experience extraordinary intimacy.

QUESTIONS

1. Read Lamentations 3:16. When was a time God broke your teeth against gravel? What did he teach you during that time?

2. Did the description of "the impostor" resonate with you? If so, in what way(s)?

3. Why is it important for a person to forgive her- or himself? Why do you imagine self-forgiveness is so hard?

4. What is the difference between incremental and trans- formational change? Why do you think couples settle for incremental instead of transformational change? Have you ever done this? Explain.

11.

NO ORDINARY SEX

I (TRISHA) AM ASSUMING some of you may have opened to this chapter before you even finished chapter one. Justin wanted to put this chapter as our opener to the book, so know you're not alone.

I think we all want to turn to this chapter if we're honest. As wives, we are desperate to understand sexual intimacy, and our husbands are desperate for us to figure it out. As Justin and I continued to surrender every page of our story, we knew that going back to understand our sexual brokenness would be part of the process. Our prayer and hope for this chapter is that you will stay open to surrendering the pages of your story in order for you to have the extraordinary sexual intimacy that your husband— I mean, that you *both*—long for.

As we identify and restore sexual brokenness, sexual satisfaction can be restored. Ordinary marriages have ordinary sex lives. Extraordinary marriages work to build intimacy and don't settle for anything less than being fully known. Anyone can have sex, but intimacy is something worth fighting for. Extraordinary sexual intimacy takes place when we restore oneness by allowing each other the right to be fully known. It transforms our understanding of the Scripture found in 1 Corinthians 7:3-4, which is often presented as saying merely that sex is a mandate for married couples, into a beautiful picture of what it means to be fully known.

> The husband should fulfill his wife's sexual needs, and the wife should fulfill her husband's needs. The wife gives authority over her body to her husband, and the husband gives authority over his body to his wife.

Our hope in writing this chapter is that your heart has already been prepared through the first ten chapters of the book to embrace this truth: extraordinary sex starts in our hearts, and as we realign our hearts with God and our spouses' hearts, a great sex life is a by-product. Justin and I had a lot to overcome in our pursuit of extraordinary sexual intimacy. We had a lot to learn about ourselves and about one another. More than telling our story, in this chapter we want to walk you through some of the things that have allowed us to heal from our own wounds and the wounds we inflicted on one another to experience the sexual intimacy we believe God had in mind for us when he created marriage.

TRISHA:

When Justin sat me down that Monday to confess to being sexually abused as a child and to a ten-year pornography addiction, at the time I was just thankful he was being completely honest with me. I wasn't thinking through the ramifications of his addiction or abuse. Honestly, there wasn't much to process because I had no clue what having a pornography addiction meant or how to heal from sexual abuse. As we started to unearth these buried pages of our stories, we realized that the lack of sexual intimacy in our relationship was the physical evidence of emotional and spiritual brokenness in our marriage.

If God was able to make us a new creation, then I had to trust that he could help us kill our old, unhealthy patterns of intimacy and create new, healthy ones to replace them. As we each unpacked the barriers to intimacy in our relationship, our lists looked very different from each other's. When sexual brokenness first took place in my life, it was under totally different circumstances than when it was broken in Justin's. We had to confess it, grieve it, and trust that the past is in the past: we can't change it, we can't get it back, but Jesus can and will somehow redeem it all.

JUSTIN:

There was no doubt that we had a lot to overcome in the area of sexual intimacy in our marriage. Even before the affair, we struggled in this area. Now the affair and my admission of being addicted to pornography had complicated an already volatile area of our marriage. We had never been on the same page sexually. How would we ever get on the same page now?

For most of our marriage, Trisha had used sexual intimacy as a weapon to get back at me, to make me pay for mistakes, to remind me that she controlled that aspect of our marriage. Because of the sexual sin in my life that had gone unconfessed and because of the sexual abuse I experienced when I was a kid, I had a very skewed view of sexual intimacy. I looked at it as an escape from reality and stress. I had the attitude that Trisha owed it to me.

What I had thought up to this point in our marriage was that our sexual issues could be solved in the bedroom. What God began to reveal to us is that our sexual brokenness and wounds needed to be healed in the living room first. As we recognized the spiritual battle we faced and as we prayed together, God restored a little more of our hearts. As truth was spoken and the waterlines of our hearts were lowered, our sexual desires and our healing increased. As Trisha and I embraced the Dip in our marriage and allowed ourselves to be more vulnerable with each other than ever before, the intimacy level in our marriage grew. And as the intimacy in our marriage grew, our sexual satisfaction grew as well.

TRISHA:

Although we knew sexual brokenness was one of the barriers to our sexual intimacy, we also knew there was more to unpack. For me, our schedule was one of my top excuses to avoid it. It was difficult to find the time and space to be intimate. I needed to have a good night's rest and a good day at home with the kids, and the moon had to align with the sun just right in order for me to be "in the mood." Sexual intimacy was somewhere in the top fifty on my to-do list. I used our schedule as an excuse not to have to be with Justin. Having three small kids and a growing ministry didn't leave a lot of room for long romantic encounters anyway, and I chose not to make it a priority. My view of the purpose it had in our relationship was so off that I was not experiencing sexual intimacy in the extraordinary. It was just another selfish "need" that Justin wanted *me* to fill.

Now seven years later, we have two teenagers and a middle schooler in the house. Not only are our schedules crazy, but theirs are too. Did I mention we have *teenagers* who stay up late and know exactly what you mean when you say you're going upstairs to go to bed? Awkward! But as God shattered our view of intimacy and created it new, we began to see not only that God was teaching us what sexual intimacy was created for, but also that we were given the parental honor to explain it to our boys.

JUSTIN:

I had been sexually abused and had never talked about it. I never dealt with it. God's intention for me had been broken by someone else, and I hid it and tried to cover it up, not because I had done anything wrong, but because of the shame and guilt that the sin committed against me had caused me to feel.

The sexual abuse I experienced caused me to equate dating and sex with acceptance and love. Because of the wounds of my past, I chose to have sex with two of the girls I dated before I met Trisha. I was trying to fix the broken part of me, and I thought relationships and sexual activity would accomplish that. Those relationships always came up void, but I never took the time to connect the dots from those relationships to a broken part of my heart.

After Trisha and I got married, because I hadn't found healing from my past, I turned to pornography to fill this void in my heart and life that the sexual brokenness had created. Each time I would engage in that activity, I would say, "I will never do that again," but it wasn't possible for me to stop on my own. I had allowed the sexual sins of my past to affect our marriage. I didn't realize it, but the choices of my past and the decisions in the present were diluting the sexual intimacy that Trisha and I were designed to experience together.

TRISHA:

It wasn't until I had to sit down with our then eleven-year-old, soon to be twelve-year-old, son that I realized my lack of sexual understanding. If I was to give a healthy, biblical view of sex to our boys, then I would have to figure it out for myself first. So I started reading. I read books like *Every Man's Battle,* by Stephen Arterburn and Fred Stoeker, and articles I found on Focus on the Family's website and even in medical journals. I was searching the Bible to try to understand the importance of sexual intimacy and not just the need to flee immorality.

If God created my husband and our boys to have wet dreams with the onset of puberty, then there had to be a purpose for those things other than causing a life of struggle with pornography and masturbation. I researched male physical anatomy, and just understanding the male body beyond what I learned in middle school was helpful. For example, wet dreams are just as natural as a girl starting her menstrual cycle. But how do you prepare your sons when the physical changes they experience have spiritual implications?

When I started reading *Every Man's Battle*, I threw the book across the room. I did *not* like what I was reading, but I forced myself to read it because my relationship with my husband and with my boys and their future wives depended on it. Although I can't say I agreed with everything in the book or that I didn't feel frustrated at the unnecessarily detailed descriptions of the authors' struggles, it did give me great insight that I didn't have before.

My biggest hurdle was trying to understand the how and why behind Justin's struggle with porn. How could I, as a woman, not fear lust, pornography, or the reality that my body will never look twenty again? Seriously, after giving birth to three kids and gaining and losing thirty pounds three different times, how on earth could I compete with the perfect-looking women on the computer screen or in the movies? How did I know that Justin wouldn't have an affair with the next best friend God placed in my life?

Then I read a powerful passage of Scripture that I had never connected with sexual struggles before:

> It's good for a man to have a wife, and for a woman
> to have a husband. Sexual drives are strong, but
> marriage is strong enough to contain them and provide
> for a balanced and fulfilling sexual life in a world of
> sexual disorder. The marriage bed must be a place of
> mutuality—the husband seeking to satisfy his wife, the
> wife seeking to satisfy her husband. Marriage is not a
> place to "stand up for your rights." Marriage is a decision
> to serve the other, whether in bed or out.
>
> I CORINTHIANS 7:2-4, *The Message*

Paul knew at least one thing about sexuality to be true: sexual drives are strong. But he says that the marriage bed is stronger. I'm not afraid to use the word *sex*, but this passage is about more than just the physical act of sex; rather, it's a beautiful definition of what extraordinary physical *intimacy* looks like. Although physical intimacy is not always *mutually desired*, when it is *mutually offered* it goes beyond the obvious physical pleasure and becomes a sacred sharing of knowing and being fully known physically, emotionally, and spiritually. Pornography, lust, and masturbation may meet one of these needs for a short period of time, but they will never fully satisfy what physical intimacy was created for.

As we unpacked these newfound truths about sexual intimacy, God was creating a new vision for Justin and me. He was giving us a pure, God-centered vision to share with our boys. I'll never forget the day that Justin took our oldest son to breakfast for "the talk." When they returned home, I was in the living room. Micah fell flat on the floor and laughed hysterically, pointing at me at the same time. Mine was more of a nervous laugh, having no idea what was so funny. After about two minutes of my asking, "What's so funny?" Micah looked up at me and said, "Dad—" giggle, giggle—"Dad told me that you guys are *active*!"

I shot Justin a look like, "What does *active* mean?" and with just one facial expression from him, I knew. We laughed until we cried!

I think the most redeeming part of choosing to go on this journey with our boys was how God used the purity with which they received the information to help Justin and me see the purity in it too. Our boys didn't have the baggage we had. They didn't squirm when we said "masturbation" because they didn't associate it as a shameful thing (even though I was *dying* every time I had to say it!). They are also aware that it's not an *if* they will be tempted sexually but *when*. They now know what to do with those temptations so as not to fall into sin. Even now with our oldest well into his teen years, although he would prefer we didn't talk about sexual issues at the dinner table, he doesn't associate embarrassment or guilt with those conversations. Our boys' vision of sex is a natural and needed part of their future marriage relationships. Physical intimacy is a gift from God.

JUSTIN & TRISHA:

BARRIERS TO INTIMACY

If we're honest, as married couples we probably had a different vision for our sex life than the reality in which we live. Maybe we thought it would be more romantic or more frequent or less stressful. We have come up against barriers. Some are physical, like weight gain or illness. For others, barriers are emotional, like low self-esteem or depression or anxiety. Sex has become something to work at rather than enjoy.

Most marriages will face barriers to sexual intimacy, which is why there are so many books and so much misinformation around about this subject. Following are two of the more critical barriers we've identified.

Sexual Impurity

One of the greatest causes of an ordinary marriage and an ordinary sex life is a lack of sexual purity. Sexual purity is receiving sexual pleasure and satisfaction only from your spouse, and giving sexual pleasure and satisfaction only to your spouse. In contrast, sexual impurity is sexual intercourse outside of marriage, sensuality, lust, and fantasizing. It is why Jesus says that if we lust in our hearts, we have committed adultery (Matthew 5:28). Sexual purity is as much about our hearts and minds as it is our bodies. Ephesians 5:3 says, "Let there be no sexual immorality, impurity, or greed among you. Such sins have no place among God's people."

A lack of sexual purity in marriage creates a huge barrier to sexual intimacy. Of course, a lack of sexual purity isn't always the result of sins that we commit. Sometimes it is the result of sins that have been committed against us.

But here's the truth: when the past isn't dealt with, it will always affect your present.

You can't experience sexual intimacy out of a heart that is sexually impure. If you are waiting on your sex life to magically get better but there is sexual impurity in your marriage, you will be waiting forever. The extraordinary sexual intimacy we desire is found in purity. For the last seven years, Trisha and I have worked hard to develop and maintain sexual purity in our relationship. It has been brutal and painful and embarrassing at times. But being fully known in our marriage has allowed us to restore sexual purity in our hearts and in our relationship.

Conflict Avoidance

I (Justin) had this assumption that did so much damage to our marriage. The assumption was that if Trisha and I had a healthy marriage, then it would be free from conflict. That isn't true at all. A healthy marriage isn't void of conflict; it is void of *unresolved* conflict. I can remember so many arguments that Trisha and I would get in, and I would say, "Just tell me what I need to apologize for!" My goal wasn't to resolve the conflict; it was to avoid it altogether.

Unresolved or avoided conflict becomes a cancer that eats away intimacy, trust, passion, and sexual attractiveness. When there is unresolved conflict in your marriage and you are ignoring it, blowing it off, or minimizing it, your spouse doesn't see you when they look at you; they see the conflict or the problem you are avoiding.

So many couples take pride in that they have never had a fight. I have to question the depth of intimacy and life that exists in a marriage that has never had conflict. When I avoid conflict or allow conflict to go unresolved, I become less trustworthy to Trisha. How can she fully trust someone who has no interest in the pain or hurt she is experiencing? Without trust, there is no foundation for intimacy. If Trisha has wounded me and I don't share that wound with her, I am communicating that I don't trust her enough with my pain to share it with her. I prove that I value counterfeit peace in our relationship more than I value being fully known.

Maybe your marriage is in an ordinary place sexually because you have been doing your best to avoid conflict. By avoiding conflict or allowing it to go unresolved, you have withheld a part of your heart from your spouse. Avoiding conflict will never foster sexual intimacy. This principle is why so many couples experience some of their most intimate moments sexually after a high level of conflict has been resolved. Unresolved conflict can be a huge barrier to physical intimacy.

STRAIGHT TALK TO LADIES

After devouring all the reading material I (Trisha) could get my hands on while on my quest to figure out what my and Justin's roles are in the area of sexual intimacy, I realized that Justin and I had to be on this journey together. I had to ask hard questions and prepare myself for uncomfortable discussions and even harder answers. As I read different material, it prompted me to ask Justin questions like:

- Do you think you watched porn because you have sexual addiction, or was it a place of escapism?
- Do make-out scenes in movies cause you to struggle?
- Do you think that "bouncing your eyes" away from sexual triggers is an effective strategy to avoid lust?

Honestly, I wish asking hard questions and being open to the ensuing discussion was a one-time thing, but for us, it's the way of life in the extraordinary. This by no means is a pass for your spouse to engage in sexual sin as long as it is confessed. Asking questions and being open for discussion means getting to the heart of the matter before it becomes an issue.

One of the struggles we often end up having tough conversations about is how Justin and I differ in our desire for physical intimacy. This seems simple to write in a sentence, but this issue could wreak havoc on our relationship if we didn't constantly keep this conversation going. Justin will most likely always desire it more than I will, but one thing we have come to recognize is that when Justin is feeling insecure about our relationship, his desire to be intimate with me is heightened. His drive at that point is a desire born out of fear, not a desire for mutual intimacy. What I have come to realize about myself is that although I really do enjoy being intimate with Justin, I left all the pursuing up to him. I have to make a conscious effort to pursue Justin as much as he pursues me, and when I don't, Justin knows he has permission to call that out in me.

We didn't choose to put this chapter at the end of the book because it's less important than the rest. Rather, sexual intimacy is of great importance, but to fully embrace the gift that God has meant for it to be in our marriages, we need to take a deeper look into matters of the heart before we bring our hearts to the bedroom.

Earlier I quoted 1 Corinthians 7:2-6. The reason this passage gives me so much hope is that God's design is stronger than the ordinary we typically settle for. Isn't it comforting to know that sex is so much more than just a physical act used to satisfy our husbands? Sex is something to look forward to, not something that is dirty, wrong, or sinful. It is a gift that God gives to a couple when they mutually and sacrificially give their bodies to one another in order to be fully known. This doesn't mean that cranky kids, the car breaking down, or a deadline at work won't get in the way of this type of intimacy. It doesn't mean that lights will automatically dim, candles will ignite, and a love song will start to play as you mutually offer yourselves to each other. What it *does* mean is that the act of offering yourself—"to serve the other, whether in bed or out"—continues to draw you to each other well after you've been sexually satisfied. And that is extraordinary.

As you confess, process, and strive for healing in the area of sexual intimacy, Satan will pounce on you to surrender to fear rather than truth. There will be days when you will have a tough conversation and walk away feeling defeated rather than enlightened or thankful for the confession spoken. There will be times you will need space to process, forgive, and pray to know what your next steps should look like to find healing. There are times even now when Justin and I find ourselves at a place of struggle in which confession alone is not enough to bring about healing. Sometimes confession will be the starting point, and you will need to seek help from a mentor, pastor, or counselor.

I pray that as you start this journey together to unpack sexual brokenness, you will not give up. I pray that you will rest in the knowledge that we are *all* flawed people. We won't get it right every time, but our hope is in knowing that Jesus will never leave us, forsake us, or abandon us. We have been given the gift of the Holy Spirit, who "helps us in our weakness" (Romans 8:26). You will have to fight for an extraordinary marriage, and each time you do, its attractiveness will outshine the dullness of life lived any other way.

STRAIGHT TALK TO GUYS

In Exodus 32, the Israelites had just witnessed God's amazing rescue from Egypt. God had fed them with a substance never seen before. He showed up in thunder around Mount Sinai and gave the people the Ten Commandments, the second of which commanded that the Israelites should never make an idol.

God's presence was powerful, God's presence was frightening, and so the people begged Moses to stand between them and God. Moses went up the mountain to meet with God. Yet when Moses spent too long on the mountain doing the work the people had given him to do, the people became antsy. They told Aaron, "Come on, make us some gods who can lead us. We don't know what happened to this fellow Moses, who brought us here from the land of Egypt" (Exodus 32:1).

The irony here is thick. The Israelites had earlier groaned to be saved from Egypt, and the Lord heard them. Egypt was a place with many gods, and one by one, God passed judgment on them all, showing his supremacy through the plagues. He brought his people through the desert, skirting the more powerful nations who were living there, in order to reveal more of himself. The Israelites recognized God's power, but they didn't recognize his lordship. It was comparatively easy to take the Israelites out of Egypt; it was much, much harder to take the Egypt out of the Israelites.

Back to the story: Aaron casts an idol of a calf using the people's jewelry. He reveals it to the cheering Israelites, who said, "O Israel, these are the gods who brought you out of the land of Egypt!" (Exodus 32:4). Aaron is swept up in the energy of the moment, and then he makes a perplexing statement: "Tomorrow will be a festival to the Lord!" (Exodus 32:5).

This would be almost comical if it weren't so disastrous. Aaron was Israel's high priest, the one who would stand between the people and God in offering sacrifices. He should have known better than to make the idol in the first place, and he certainly should have known better than to mention the Lord and then worship an idol. The First Commandment, after all, was to have no other gods. That Aaron could remember the Lord's name (and thus probably his commandment) yet indulge in idol worship is telling: there is often a disconnect between what we say we believe and what we do. We can attempt to change our behaviors, but without a change of heart, these changes are in vain.

And that is the problem as we talk about sexual purity. For ten years, I worshiped God on Sundays, taught God's Word, and led people spiritually, yet I had allowed sexual sin and brokenness to be a part of my life. It is so easy to say, "Don't lust. Don't look at pornography. Don't fantasize about other women. Don't compromise your sexual purity." It's easy to call those behaviors out in one another, and we can do our best to try to live up to that standard, but if our hearts don't change, then we will struggle and fail in this area over and over again. We will become prisoners to our own sexual sins.

There have been so many times in our marriage that Trisha and I would hear a speaker talking about sexual purity, and Trisha would ask me if I struggled in that area. "No, I don't struggle with that," I'd say. "I struggle with pride and arrogance (and lying). That is my battleground, not sexual purity."

After the affair, I found myself needing a lot more than just my behavior to change. I had spent ten years promising myself I wouldn't look at porn anymore, yet I continued to do it. I had always had great intentions; I just wasn't intentional in allowing my heart to change. My intentions weren't going to be the measurement anymore. I had to choose differently now.

The first choice I made was to stop deceiving myself. I was able to lie to Trisha so easily because I had lied to myself first. For us as guys, to have the sexual intimacy we desire with our wives, we have to refuse to lie to ourselves. Here are some of the lies we often tell ourselves:

- I'm just window shopping. I'm not buying.
- No one is getting hurt by my looking at porn. It doesn't affect me like it affects other guys.
- I can stop anytime I want.
- I can manage my lust, my thoughts, and my desires.
- It's not that big of a deal; I'm just flirting.
- I don't need to talk to anyone about it; I can handle it.
- The movies I watch aren't that bad; they could be a lot worse.

The problem for us is that our capacity to compartmentalize our lives is amazing. We have the capacity to say we are deeply in love with our wives and yet at the same time deeply desire another woman's body. In our minds, those two things have nothing to do with each other. But in reality, they have everything to do with each other. If you want to find the path to sexual purity so you can experience sexual intimacy, you have to stop deceiving yourself. You need to admit your struggles, weaknesses, addictions, and sins. I don't know what that looks like for you, but for me it meant getting help.

What I realized is that porn wasn't my problem. What kept me in bondage to a sexual addiction was pride. It was a lack of surrender. My pride wouldn't allow me to admit my problem. My pride wouldn't allow me to seek help. My pride was more important than submitting to Christ and to my wife. My pride was bigger than my porn problem. My pride kept my porn problem big.

Shortly after our family moved away from Genesis Church, I began a nine-week program to break free from my addiction to pornography. Trisha and I had honest and open conversations about my struggles and about things that trigger my desires and how she could help me and pray for me. It was uncomfortable for me to be up at two in the morning talking about pornography and masturbation with my wife. But in order to have a different marriage, we had to start doing things differently. I continued to go to counseling to talk through my abuse issues and sexual brokenness.

If you want to change this aspect of your heart and not just alter your behavior, you must guard your heart and mind. As we come to terms with the battle that we as men fight every day, it is a battle for our hearts and a battle for our minds. It is not nearly as important to monitor our behavior as it is to guard our minds.

Philippians 4:8 says, "Brothers and sisters, whatever is true, whatever is noble, whatever is right, whatever is pure, whatever is lovely, whatever is admirable—if anything is excellent or praiseworthy—think about such things" (NIV).

At the beginning of our separation, our counselor challenged me to fast from television until Trisha and I reconciled. My initial response was, "Like, not even Sports Center?" I was willing to do anything, so I agreed. For the next two months, I didn't watch any TV. I spent so much more time praying and so much more time in God's Word. I realized how many of my thoughts weren't centered on what was true, noble, right, pure, lovely, admirable, excellent, or praiseworthy.

Here is what's wild: I used to teach this passage on Sunday mornings. I quoted this passage to guys I met with who had pornography addictions. I often shared this verse with friends I played basketball with who couldn't stop cussing. I knew this passage, but I didn't apply it. Well, I guess I applied it to the point that it felt comfortable, but not when it conflicted with *CSI: Miami* or *Grey's Anatomy*. I never quoted it when I was trying to talk Trisha into watching an R-rated movie that "only has one sex scene that we can fast-forward through." I never broke out this verse as I was walking into the movie theater to watch a movie I knew had sexual content and nudity. I knew this verse was true, but I didn't take seriously the consequences of not applying it to my life.

Wherever sin lives, intimacy dies. That is true in your relationship with God, and it is true in your marriage. But the good news is that wherever intimacy lives, sin dies. This isn't meant to be an indictment of what you watch on TV or the movies you see. But for Trisha and me, we watch very little network TV. We attend very few movies these days. That is a price we have chosen to pay. Even saying it is a "price" feels weird. The people who have the hardest time with our decision and who make fun of us the most are Christians. They feel that because we choose not to go to movies with nudity, we are saying we are holier than they are. My response is, "I'm not saying I'm holier than you; I know I'm not holy. I know I don't want to place my heart and mind in that situation because I know how easy it is to fall."

Making this decision has paid off in so many ways. When our oldest son, Micah, turned twelve years old, he had some friends over for a birthday party. They played video games for a while, and then they wanted me to take them to the movies. They started talking about different movies to see, what movies some of them had seen, and what was good and what wasn't. I just prayed that God would give me the wisdom I needed to help my son navigate the situation.

Here is the cool part: we have talked so much about this principle of purity and how to protect our hearts that I didn't have to say anything. Micah went to the Plugged In website and reviewed all of the movies that were playing. He then told his friends the two or three movies that he would feel comfortable watching. End of discussion. It won't always be that cut and dried, but that is just one instance of "whatever is pure, whatever is holy, whatever is right" paying off in a big, big way. And when we set the pace and tone, others will follow, in our households and even outside them.

* * *

We are still on this journey. There are seasons of our relationship when we are on the same page and we are in tune with one another and we feel like our level of intimacy is high and our sex life is extraordinary. Then there are seasons of life that bring uncertainty and anxiety and busyness and ordinary. One of us feels neglected or misunderstood. Our differences in this area are often more prevalent than our desire to be on the same page. We have to constantly choose to start the conversation all over again. We have to choose to remind ourselves of truth. We have to choose oneness in this area, because none of us drift toward oneness.

The oneness that God desires for you is daily under attack. You will have to fight for it. You will have to fight for each other. You will have to be intentional. Extraordinary isn't about how many times you have sex in a week; it is how passionately you are pursuing oneness and intimacy. It is in that pursuit that our sexual desires are not only met, but also satisfied.

QUESTIONS

1. Before you got married, what role did you believe sexual intimacy played in a marriage? In what ways was your belief right or wrong?

2. What do you feel are the greatest barriers to sexual intimacy in your marriage? Why do these barriers exist?

3. On a scale of 1 to 10, how well do you understand your spouse in this area? What questions do you have for your spouse?

4. Surrender is a beautiful but scary word to embrace. What do you need to surrender in order to fully embrace the role God intended for sexual intimacy in your marriage relationship?

12.

NO ORDINARY MARRIAGE

WHEN WE WALKED into the Ritz-Carlton hotel in the Grand Cayman Islands, I (Justin) knew we would never go back into vocational ministry. After two months of working at P. F. Chang's, I was offered a job at a recruiting firm. It was a commission-only job, which meant if I didn't close a deal, I wouldn't get paid. But there was no limit to how much I could earn if I could figure out how to be an executive recruiter. "Executive recruiter" is a fancy way of saying "headhunter." Companies would pay me a fee for placing employees with their organizations. I had no idea people found jobs through recruiters. I thought that was what Monster and CareerBuilder were for.

There is a high turnover rate in the executive recruiting field due to the commission-only pay structure and that all sales are over the phone. So as a rookie, my job was to make eighty to one hundred calls a day and hope that I could find companies that needed employees, then find employees who were qualified for those jobs and willing to explore new opportunities. Most rookies last sixty to ninety days. At that point they either get it and start closing deals or get frustrated and move on.

It had been a year and two months since I started, and by God's grace, I had figured it out. Not only did I figure it out, I was the highest-producing rookie in the country. In my first year, I had earned just about every award you could earn, including President's Club, which gave Trisha and me an all-expenses-paid trip to the Grand Caymans with other high producers at our firm. God was good—and so was being out of ministry.

When we walked into the hotel, tears filled my eyes. I knew there was no way I could ever make up to Trisha for all that we had been through, but we were a little more than a year into our recovery, and this trip was confirmation that we were going to make it, that God's best was in front of us and not behind us. I said to her, "If a million people showed up at our church, they wouldn't send us to the Grand Caymans on an incentive trip. I could get used to life outside of ministry."

We sat on the beach and drank fufu drinks. We sat next to the pool and drank fufu drinks. We walked and talked and enjoyed being with each other in a way that we never had before. It was like being on the cruise again, except we were living as a brand-new Justin and Trisha. One of the things we talked about on that vacation was how much of the journey I had missed because I was so focused on the destination. I had spent the past ten years building something. I was building a student ministry, building a reputation, building a bank account, building an image, building a leadership structure, building an organization, building a church.

None of those things are bad, but the focus I had of "what's next" usually caused me to miss the pleasure of "what's now." I hadn't enjoyed the journey because I was so focused on the next destination. Arriving was more important to me than becoming. As we sat on the beach and talked, there was no doubt we still had healing to experience, but I had joy in my heart. For the first time as an adult, I was joyful.

One of the goals of this book has been to help you give Jesus more of your heart and more of your marriage. Only Jesus can restore the joy you had when you said, "I do." When you are pursuing the destination more passionately than you pursue the journey, you are likely to miss both. Intimacy, being fully known, is experienced as we find joy in the journey and not just in the destination. We were finally understanding that and living with joy.

TRISHA:

After moving to Zionsville, Justin and I went back and forth about attending church. I was in a great place with Jesus, just not with his bride. We continued to watch church online for a while, but then we took a leap of faith and went to Eagle Church because . . . well, it was convenient, being right across the street. It was the first time we walked into a church without one person knowing who we were. It was bittersweet to be anonymous. It was great to worship without added responsibility, while at the same time we felt incredibly lonely.

If I had known what God was up to when he brought Eagle Church into our lives, I'm certain I wouldn't have gone.

After a year of just attending, Micah was now old enough to be part of the youth group, so I decided to volunteer in whatever capacity they needed because in my mind students were *safe*. In 2008 I was talked into going to a conference in Orlando with a group of our high school students. There my whole "students are safe" theory was blown to smithereens.

These kids were not safe at all! They loved me with reckless love. They tapped into a place of my heart surrounded by caution tape with a large sign that said, "You will be shot if you enter this area!" but they didn't care. God used these students, our youth pastors, and the other adult volunteers on this trip to soften my heart for a message God was about to pour over me.

One morning at the conference, I sat in a room along with three thousand students and youth leaders. I listened to this pastor I had never heard of before talk about God's greatness and his "crazy love" for us. As Francis Chan spoke, I could feel my heart beating so hard I thought I might be having a heart attack. My sweet friend Mary could tell I was struggling and put her hand on my back. My body temperature rose and I started sweating. I went from anger to panic—and the conversation began.

God, don't do this to me! I don't want to be called or affirmed back into ministry! Please don't break my heart for what breaks yours! I can't do it! I want to enjoy President's Club trips with Justin—because they are safe!

After Francis Chan finished speaking, a missionary from the missionary conference that was going on at the same time rose to speak. The man shared a story about himself and his wife and their three small kids purchasing fruit at a small market somewhere in Africa. He stayed in their Jeep with all three kids in the back as his wife got out to purchase fruit. As she glanced over the selection of fruit, three armed gunmen approached the Jeep. When she looked up to see where the commotion was coming from, she saw the gunmen jump her husband, throw him out of the Jeep, and take off with all three children in the back.

At this point, I was trying so hard to hold back tears that my head began to hurt. My anger had almost become a boiling rage. *God, why on earth am I listening to this? Do you seriously want me to not like you? If these children die in this story, I'm out of here!* My heart already felt fragile from the unexpected thoughts and emotions this trip was unlocking; it never crossed my mind that God would use this trip to call us back into ministry.

The missionary continued to share that after stealing the Jeep, the gunmen realized they were headed straight for a police post, so they turned around and drove back by the fruit stand, and as they did, the missionary desperately ran after the Jeep, jumped on it with feet dragging, and managed to pull only one of his children out of the back as the gunmen took off with the other two. He paused, took a deep breath (as did I), and said that during all of this, his wife—while tearfully watching her children taken captive—shared with those around her that although she may lose her children, "they will be in the most glorious place with a heavenly Father who will love them so much more than they could be loved here on earth. This heavenly Father longs for you to be with him too. All he asks is for you to believe in him."

The missionary finished his story and told us that about a mile down the road, for some unknown reason, the gunmen threw the other two children out of the Jeep unharmed. The audience released a collective sigh of relief, and the missionary finished by saying, "The call of God on your life is not about the destination but about who you are becoming along the way." I spent the next two years trying to figure out what exactly that meant.

JUSTIN:

I believed moving from Noblesville to Zionsville meant starting over. In many ways, we did start over, but my hope was that we could leave the past in the past and not share it with anybody. It didn't mean that we wouldn't deal with it, just that it was our story and should stay our story.

The problem was that God didn't see it the same way I did.

As our life outside of ministry continued, we lived with the tension of Trisha feeling called back into ministry and with God bringing individuals and couples into our lives who had heard our story or just felt drawn to share their marriage problems with us. We began to meet with couples over coffee or dinner, and they would just pour out their hearts to us. God used our experience to give them hope and a plan to pursue healing for themselves. That felt right. I knew God couldn't (or wouldn't) use me in vocational ministry again, but it was amazing to see God redeem our story in the lives of these hurting couples. I was comfortable allowing God to use us in small, unnoticeable ways.

God continued to use Brennan Manning's *Abba's Child* to utterly destroy any preconceived notions I had of him and of our future as a family. One of the things Manning said in that book seemed very relevant to where we were:

> In a futile attempt to erase our past, we deprive the community of our healing gift. If we conceal our wounds out of fear and shame, our inner darkness can neither be illuminated nor become a light for others.

The question we had to ask ourselves was, would we allow our past to be a healing gift to others? Or would we conceal our wounds out of fear and shame? One day I was willing; the next I was terrified. One day I could see what God was calling us to; the next I was convinced I was manipulating God and Trisha again to get back into ministry. There was so much work left to do in my heart. I had no idea where to start or what to do next. God would have to orchestrate this because I wasn't willing to pursue it without him.

In August 2008, I met with Kerry, the senior pastor at Eagle. Kerry and his wife, Melissa, had become trusted friends. They had spent over two years encouraging Trisha and me and providing a safe place for us to heal. Kerry and I had shared meals and conversations talking about our journey, and he knew of our love (and at times hatred) of ministry. Trisha and I had talked to Melissa and him about Trisha's experience in Orlando and the call she felt back into ministry, but we didn't know what to do with that.

I walked into his office and he spun around in his chair to face me. If there was small talk, I don't remember it. What I do remember is a game-changing statement he made: "I've seen the restoration journey you've been on in your marriage. I've seen the influence you've had with couples here at Eagle. I believe in you.

I believe God isn't done with you. I'd like to help you find complete restoration and healing back into ministry."

Lots of thoughts flooded my mind: *I'm not worthy. I'm not qualified. I'm not ready. I'm not sure our marriage can handle that. I'm not sure I can handle that. What if I fail again? What if I hurt people again?*

I told Kerry I didn't know where to start or how such a thing was even possible. Kerry said he would be willing to walk with us through the process. He introduced a plan that would involve my commitment for up to a year. It started with two things.

First, Trisha and I had to be willing to dream again. One of the things God revealed to us is that we are dreamers. We love to dream together. We started out with dreams of what God had in store for us, and slowly those dreams shifted to ministry and the church. But in our years of ordinary marriage, we had almost lost our ability to dream for ourselves and for one another. At this point in our journey, I felt as though I wasn't allowed to dream again. I had messed up so bad that I had forfeited any dream that God had for me and that I could have for myself. It was a life-giving process to dream again about my life, my future, our marriage, our kids, and what God might do through us as we chose to step out again and follow him.

Second, I had to be willing to seek reconciliation with those I had wounded. When Trisha and I left Genesis, we left for good. We never went back. We cut all ties. We followed the advice of our counselor that the best thing for them and for our marriage was to completely disconnect from them. Now, almost three years later, I was being asked to seek out the leaders, staff members, and some attendees of the church and ask for forgiveness. That seemed self-serving to me. "I know I haven't talked to you in three years," I imagined myself saying, "but I want to go back into ministry, and in order to do that, I need to meet with you." That seemed like the old Justin. That seemed manipulative, and I wanted no part of it. God was going to have to intervene.

A few days after I met with Kerry, I got a call from one of the elders at Genesis. We hadn't spoken in several months, and his call was totally out of the blue. He told me of a marriage issue one of our friends at the church was facing. He said, "I know we haven't talked in a while, but you are uniquely qualified to help. Would you meet with them?" I told him I would do whatever I could.

That afternoon Trisha went over to their house, and that evening I met with them too. God used that situation over the next six months to strategically reconnect me with every leader and staff member at Genesis. When I say every leader and staff member, that doesn't include Trisha's best friend and her husband. When Trisha's letter went without response, she felt she had been faithful in seeking reconciliation and to this day has left the timing and healing up to God. But that didn't prevent us from walking through the relational doors God opened.

We shared meals. We went out for coffee. We talked on the phone. I asked them to forgive me and told them how sorry I was for how much I had hurt them. I was able to share with them the painful yet redemptive journey Trisha and I had been on the past two and a half years. I had the opportunity to personally thank them for loving us well and leading the church with such integrity and obedience. It was painful and sad and emotional and remorseful and beautiful and redemptive and healing all at the same time. God had come through again and provided us with another step in our healing and in the reconciliation of so many broken relationships.

TRISHA:

As Justin and I embraced this intense yet redeeming path back into ministry, we still had no idea what "going back into ministry" would look like. In the past, I had always assumed "calling" was defined by a title or position meant just for pastors. I had convinced myself that being "called" back into ministry was God's way of completing our redemption story. I looked at it as a bookend rather than another chapter. I couldn't have been more wrong!

This process wasn't about trying to earn grace. This wasn't about proving we were worthy to be back in ministry. Justin and I were being asked to be willing to have a posture of submission in order for God to bring about transformation in areas of our hearts that were still wrapped in caution tape. Look at what the Bible says in Hebrews 12:10-11:

> For our earthly fathers disciplined us for a few years,
> doing the best they knew how. But God's discipline is
> always good for us, so that we might share in his holiness.
> No discipline is enjoyable while it is happening—it's
> painful! But afterward there will be a peaceful harvest of
> right living for those who are trained in this way.

We sometimes confuse discipline with a lack of grace, but discipline is an extension of grace. Being willing to submit to a process that is good allows us to "share in his holiness." Submitting to the restoration process was giving Kerry and the others involved permission to help take the tape off our hearts and expose the pain we had not yet dealt with.

The writer of Hebrews says, "No discipline is enjoyable while it is happening—it's painful!" It *was* hard to watch Justin apologize to those he had hurt. It *was* hard that even though I had forgiven Justin, others still hadn't. It *was* hard to not defend Justin but rather to allow God to heal those still hurting. It *was* hard to relinquish my caution tape that made me feel safe and protected in order to receive apologies made to me and to give them to others. It was painful, "but afterward there will be a peaceful harvest of right living for those who are trained in this way." As we embraced this truth, God continued to create anew the calling we had allowed to die.

In January 2009, lead pastor Aaron Brockett of Traders Point

Christian Church asked if we would share our story at their week-end services. Traders Point was also in Zionsville, so sharing meant that many of the people in the congregation would know us but not our story. I said no, but Justin asked if I would pray about it and make sure I was saying no for the right reason, not just out of fear. I prayed and felt God prompting me to share our story. I told Pastor Brockett I would do it "just this once." So in January 2009, Justin and I invited two-thousand-plus people into our story. I was not prepared for the response that followed.

After the first service, there was a long line of people waiting to talk to us. I didn't understand why they would want advice from us after hearing our story. After the last service, Justin and I talked to so many people that we had to ask a family friend to come to the church to pick up our bored-out-of-their-minds kids and take them home because it was so late in the afternoon. The people who came up to us wanted to know how we stayed married, how I forgave Justin, how Justin forgave himself, how I learned to trust again. At that time, I didn't really have an answer other than taking it day by day. We naively put our e-mail in the bulletin for anyone who wanted to talk, and for the next month, we responded to and met with so many people. It was exhausting.

Justin called Pete to ask for advice. Pete knew about my experience in Orlando and the journey we were on to go back into ministry. Every couple of months, Pete would text or call to offer Justin a job at his church, Cross Point Community Church. It became a running joke between us all that there was no way Pete could get me to move to Nashville again. He couldn't get me to move to the Grand Cayman Islands, for that matter, because I wasn't moving anywhere!

Justin told Pete about the response we received after sharing our story and asked for direction about what to do. He encouraged us to start a blog. Justin's response was, "What's a blog?" We were so out of the loop in social media that we weren't reading blogs, we weren't on Twitter, and I had just joined Facebook in 2008.

So in January 2009, we created RefineUs.org and, from our blog, RefineUs Ministries. God gave us a burden not just for marriages that were failing but also for seemingly healthy marriages that were really just ordinary.

At this point we had several opportunities to return to vocational ministry, and they all seemed good. We were asked to consider starting a church in Chicago. We were asked to consider starting another church in Indianapolis. We considered raising money and working for RefineUs full time. As we prayed and agonized about the different ministry opportunities to choose from, Pete's invitation to come on staff at Cross Point, while it didn't make much sense and scared me to death, felt like the right one. Although Justin felt like he would one day return to being a lead pastor, we both felt it was too soon (at least for us) for Justin to take on such a position. So in July 2009, Justin accepted the Campus and Teaching Pastor position at Cross Point, and we prepared to move to Nashville—again.

JUSTIN:

When I chose to pursue an extraordinary life with God and an extraordinary marriage, God brought healing to parts of my story and marriage that I didn't even know had been wounded.

About a week before we moved from Zionsville to Nashville, I got a call from my mom, asking if she could spend the afternoon with me. Trisha was in Nashville painting the house we were renting, and our two oldest boys were at basketball camp. I let her know that it was just Isaiah and me at the house and that she was welcome to come hang out.

From the time she arrived, I knew something was off. I didn't know what, but she wasn't acting like herself. A few months before, my mom and dad had finalized their divorce after thirty-six years of marriage. I knew how much my mom had been through and at first just attributed her demeanor to the pain of her own situation. As she prepared to leave, she asked if we could sit down and talk.

She became very emotional. We both sat down on the couch, and she took a Bible out of her bag.

She said, "The past few months have been some of the most difficult of my entire life. I have spent them encouraging your dad to be a man of truth. To be honest. To live with integrity. The more I have gone after your dad to tell the truth, the more God has convicted me of choices I have made to not be a person of truth. One of the things God has laid on my heart is my relationship with you. I am going to tell you right now, Justin, that I am laying our relationship on the altar. I am willing to sacrifice our relationship to do what is right and to be a person of truth." With that statement, she opened the Bible to Genesis 22, where the story of Abraham taking Isaac up the mountain and putting him on the altar is recorded.

I'm a hypochondriac, so at this point I wasn't hearing anything my mom was saying. I was thinking, *She is going to sacrifice me? Do I have a deadly disease that she hasn't told me about? I wonder how advanced it is? I wonder how much time I have left? If I were to die, where would they bury me? We haven't even bought a cemetery plot yet! I hope it isn't a painful death. I'm really too young to die!* I know, I have serious issues, but that was my thought process. After I snapped out of it, my mom got to the point.

She said, "You know that your dad and I got married fifteen days after you were born. I got pregnant with you out of wedlock." I nodded. "What you don't know and what I have been lying to you about for the past thirty-six years is that when I met your dad, I was eight months pregnant with you. Your dad is not your real dad. Your dad adopted you when you were a toddler. He is your adoptive father, not your birth father."

My head started spinning. She could have told me I was from Mars and it would have made more sense to me than what she was saying. I don't remember much of what else she said, but I do remember asking her to leave. As soon as she was in the car, I called Trisha and told her of the bomb that had just been dropped on me. She couldn't make any more sense of it than I could. The identity

I had found in ministry for so many years was gone, and now the identity I had found in my parents was turned upside down.

Trisha was just a few minutes from Pete and Brandi's house, so she drove there and shared the news with them while she was on the phone with me. Pete got on the phone, and the first thing he said was, "Well, if ministry doesn't work out for you, you could always go on Jerry Springer." It was the light moment we all needed. Then he said something profound: "It is all out now. There is absolutely nothing hidden about your life anymore."

That statement became the foundation for another work of healing and restoration that continues today. The way God had led Trisha through the process of forgiving me was crucial as I walked through that same process with my mom. It was a yearlong process of asking questions, having tough conversations, choosing to forgive, and allowing truth to bring healing. Today, my mom and I have a deeper, closer relationship than we've ever had. The waterline is completely lowered. There is nothing left below the surface.

JUSTIN & TRISHA:

FINAL WORDS FROM TRISHA

I wish I could say that it was all happily ever after, but there is no pretty bow to tie around our refinement process. Six months into our move to Nashville, I became depressed and had no idea why, so I went back to counseling. As I unpacked my heart with Justin and my counselor, I realized that I had made Cross Point the Promised Land where life was to be easy-breezy 24-7.

When reality set in that our return to ministry was going to be harder than I realized, I felt lost. I had convinced myself that ministry wouldn't be as hard this time around because *we* were different, so ministry had to be too. I apologized to both Pete and Brandi for placing unrealistic expectations on them and on Cross Point. I had to allow the principles I had learned for my marriage relationship to be transferred to my relationship with the bride of Christ. Three years later, the bride of Christ has become a good friend that I get to partner with to share the love of Christ with others.

As you choose to take the path to extraordinary, know that there will be discouraging days when you take three steps forward, then two steps back. All the principles we have learned and shared throughout this book are principles we must still remind ourselves of and continue to explore. The biggest lesson I have learned writing this book is that just because you have the knowledge of something doesn't mean you automatically apply it to your life and allow it to transform you. Living in the extraordinary is daily asking God to lead us out of the ordinary we are tempted to settle for. If I had to go through all the pain and trials again in order to lead me to who I am today, I would do it in a heartbeat. I'm eternally grateful to our heavenly Father, who loves us so much that he gave us the extraordinary gift of his Son so that we could have an extraordinary life through him.

FINAL WORDS FROM JUSTIN

Just a few nights ago, I sat on the couch next to Trisha, fighting to stay awake while we watched TV. Seven years ago, we were fighting for our married lives. I was fighting to be a person of truth. Trisha was fighting to forgive. We were fighting for a new start. What was true then is still true today: we aren't meant to fight *with* each other; we are meant to fight *for* each other. I would never choose the path we took, but I wouldn't change it either. It was and is worth the fight.

God is fighting for you right now. God is fighting for your heart. God is fighting for your husband. God is fighting for your wife. God's vision for your marriage is extraordinary! Don't stop fighting. Don't stop pursuing. Don't stop sharing truth. Don't stop forgiving. Don't stop praying. Don't lose hope. The vision you had when you said "I do" isn't nearly as extraordinary as God's vision for your marriage.

Author Frederick Buechner says, "A marriage made in Heaven is one where a man and a woman become more richly themselves together than the chances are either of them could ever have managed to become alone."

Beyond ordinary is you becoming more of who God has created you to be so you can become more of the husband or wife God calls you to be. As you choose refinement and allow Christ to transform you, your marriage will move beyond ordinary.

God's vision for your marriage is oneness.

It is possible, but it has to be intentional.

You have to choose it, day after day, moment after moment. One step at a time.

QUESTIONS

1. Have you ever had God call you out of a place of comfort and into a place of risk? How did you react?

2. Do you see your marriage story as something God could use to bring hope to others? Why or why not?

3. In order to begin an extraordinary marriage you will have to ask God daily to lead you out of the ordinary you are tempted to settle for. Moving forward, what will you refuse to settle for?

4. God's vision for your marriage is oneness. What will you do today to pursue oneness with your spouse?

Acknowledgments

FROM JUSTIN

Tony and Suzy Anthony—Thank you for looking past your own hurt and giving me a place to live, heal, and allow God to restore my soul.

Mike and Emily Jackson—Thank you for loving me in spite of the pain I caused you. Your grace and mercy in my darkest hours helped me find my way out of the darkness.

Craig Parker, Dave Rodriguez, Keith Carlson—Thank you for tough love, speaking truth, and pastoring my family even as you shared in the consequences of my poor choices.

Mom—Your willingness to lower the waterline in our relationship and to be honest and vulnerable allowed God's grace and mercy to shine brightly. Thank you for loving me and my family well.

Brennan Manning—You will probably never see this thank-you, but I had to acknowledge the role *Abba's Child* had in my redemption and restoration. Thank you.

Bill and Martha Kuntz—Thank you for taking a chance on a broken-down pastor that had never done sales before by allowing me to be a part of PrincetonOne. God used you to help me provide for my family as he healed my heart and prepared us for ministry.

FROM TRISHA

Mom—The trials and heartaches which have flowed from your life would leave most people defeated and bitter, but not you. Your very being is a testimony that through Christ all things are possible if we let him lead. Thank you for choosing him over and over and over again. You will never know how deep and far reaching your testimony has moved others closer to Jesus. Thank you for being beyond ordinary. I love you!

Pops—Thank you for loving me and believing in my marriage when I couldn't do either for myself.

Angi, Jodi, and Brooker (Team Justin)—For telling our waiter his name isn't Justin and for simply being you!

Rose Curnutt, Beth Belleville, and Julie Gerhardt—Thank you for loving my boys and me in the midst of the storm and for telling me that one day God was going to use our mess for his glory.

Joan Jackson—Thank you for your wisdom and love. I will forever cherish my days of Bible study in your home!

Kathy Elzinga—Thank you for being an unseen superhero who dared to park outside my home dressed in the full armor of God to be a prayer warrior fighting for my family.

Frankie—As my brother, it came as no surprise that you came to my rescue when I needed you most. But the day you chose to see and hug Justin just hours into our chaos forever changed my perspective of grace. Thank you!

Natalie Grant—Your music provided a backdrop to my pain that often guided me back to the truth of who God is. Thank you for your passion for your music, your family, and your friends.

Charity Martin—I never knew sweet tea and homemade peanut butter cookies would touch my heart so deeply. Thank you!

Lindsey Nobles—Without even asking you took it upon yourself to bust through walls I had built around my heart. You have given me the gift to see that truth, grace, and trust can coexist, even in the messiness of life and friendships! I love you!

JUSTIN & TRISHA

Lisa Jackson—Your belief in us and in this book gave us confidence and endurance throughout this entire project. Thank you for choosing us and for developing us as authors. Thank you for enduring my (Justin's) long-winded conference calls and incessant e-mails. We appreciate you so much.

Jonathan Schindler—Thank you for the time, heart, and attention to detail you gave our manuscript. You said you had three goals: to preserve the author's voice, to edify the reader, and to bring glory to God. We believe with all of our hearts that you accomplished all three with our book. Thank you for your patience and care with our story.

To our Tyndale team: *Kara, April, Maria, Carol, Linda, Jennifer, and the rest of the Beers team*—Thank you for helping us share such an intimate story in a way that shows God's grace and restoration. We love you and appreciate you so very much.

Jenni Burke—Thank you for your guidance, encouragement, gentle spirit, and tenacious belief in this book and in us. Thank you for responding to text messages . . . even when I (Trish) told Justin not to send them. We are blessed to have you not only as our literary agent but also as our friend.

Don Jacobson—Thank you for your heart for authors, their stories, and the way you steward the role, experience, and authority God has given you. It is an honor to be represented by you.

Our family: *Julie, Frankie, Justin, Josh, Meredith, Jake, Deb, Jonah, Crystal, our dads, and our awesome nieces and nephews*—Thank you for your continued love and support. We love you deeply!

Pete and Brandi—There are no words to describe the depth of love and gratitude we have for you. Over the past twelve years, you have listened, loved, supported, encouraged, admonished, believed in, and inspired us to be the family we are today. Without you, this book wouldn't exist. Thank you for being beyond-ordinary friends who love unconditionally.

Our Cross Point Community Church family—Thank you for truly being a place where "Everyone's welcomed because nobody's perfect and anything is possible"! Not all churches give second chances. Thank you for the honor of pastoring again at Cross Point.

Tom and Shelly Anthony—Thank you for your unconditional love, words of wisdom, encouragement, and friendship. Your shoulders to cry on have guided us in times of doubt and carried us in times of fear. This book has our friendship sprinkled from cover to cover.

Chris and Cindy Johnson—Beyond ordinary is the only way to describe the friendship that you have given us over the past ten years. You are our biggest cheerleaders and dearest friends.

Dan Crosley—Thank you for setting us on a narrow, painful, and hard path that led us to a marriage that is beyond ordinary.

Our neighbors on Lancaster Place—Your love of our family broke down walls and healed wounds you didn't even knew existed. Thank you for being biblical community when we needed it most.

Focus on the Family—Thank you for your ministry that provides crisis counseling in people's most desperate time of need, and thank you to the counselor, whose name we don't even know, whose words of wisdom changed everything.

Aaron Brockett—Thank you for hearing the story within us before we even knew how to articulate it. Sunday, January 4, 2009, launched a bigger story that God is still writing to this day.

Eagle Church—Thank you for providing a safe place to hide and heal yet loving us out of hiding to share our healing with the world.

Pam Case—Your vivacious passion to see people win is contagious! Thank you for coming alongside us and for opening doors for this book to have a fighting chance.

Bryan Norman—Thank you for your brilliance, friendship, and belief in us. Thank you for lunches full of Mexican food and grace.

Kenny Sandifer—Thank you for being our counselor and friend who keeps us on the path of an extraordinary marriage when we feel like we have lost our way.

Pam, Emily, and Rachel—Thank you for many years of being family away from family. We love you!

Readers of RefineUs—Thank you for being a part of our ministry. Who says a blog can't change the world! Every marriage that is helped with this book is a reflection of God's using you as a part of our community and ministry. We are grateful for your years of support and encouragement.

Notes

CHAPTER 1
21 *ex•traor•di•nary: Merriam-Webster's Collegiate Dictionary*, 11th ed.

CHAPTER 2
44 *less than 8 percent of Christian couples say that they pray together on a regular basis:* Dennis Rainey, "The Secret to a Lasting Marriage," http://www.familylife.com/articles/topics/marriage/staying-married/growing-spiritually/the-secret-to-a-lasting-marriage.

CHAPTER 4
78 *Almost everything in life worth doing . . . changing the rules as they go:* Seth Godin, *The Dip* (New York: Portfolio, 2007), 16–17, 19.

CHAPTER 6
111 *Our direction . . . our destination:* Andy Stanley, *The Principle of the Path* (Nashville: Thomas Nelson, 2008), 136.

CHAPTER 9
166 *Not forgiving . . . the rat to die:* Anne Lamott, *Traveling Mercies* (New York: Anchor Books, 1999), 134.

CHAPTER 10
170 *When Christ calls . . . come and die:* Dietrich Bonhoeffer, *The Cost of Discipleship* (New York: Touchstone, 1995), 11.
178 *My identity as Abba's child . . . their life situations:* Brennan Manning, *Abba's Child* (Colorado Springs: NavPress, 1994, 2002), 71.
178 *The betrayals and infidelities . . . confused:* Ibid., 72.

185 *God whispers . . . deaf world:* C.S. Lewis, *The Problem of Pain* (New York: HarperCollins, 1940/1996), 91.

CHAPTER 12

210 *In a futile attempt to erase our past, . . . become a light for others:* Manning,

219 *A marriage made in Heaven . . . could ever have managed to become alone:* Frederick Buechner, *Whistling in the Dark* (New York: HarperCollins Publishers, 1993), 87.

RESTORING HOPE | RENEWING RELATIONSHIPS

JUSTIN & TRISHA DAVIS are the founders of RefineUs Ministries, an organization started as a response to the call and passion God placed in their hearts for marriage and families.

RefineUs has a mission of restoring hope and renewing relationships. Through their blog (refineus.org), their marriage coaching program (CoachUs), and their marriage mentoring program (MentorUs) they hope to move couples closer to unity as they individually move closer to Christ.

Justin and Trisha travel and speak to a variety of audiences. Whether they are talking with a couple over a cup of coffee or a couple of thousand people in a church service, they passionately share God's vision for every marriage to move beyond ordinary.

refineus.org